Distant Days

Denny H. Lincoln

Tallis Press

Author's Note

Following the successful publication in 1997 of **Distant Days** concerning the villages of Elloughton cum Brough and Brantingham I was persuaded by a number of people to write another local history book on the nearby South Cave and North Cave areas. Some eighteen months have been spent in researching for material for this new book, much of it provided through the generosity of local inhabitants of these villages. Not only have they given me a great deal of their time relating their memories of a bygone age but out of boxes, family albums, drawers and even sheds, a rich collection of interesting and rare pictures have emerged, many being printed in this book for the first time. The majority of the photographs were taken during the first half of the 20th century when life in these four villages had a distinctly quieter pace from that of today. Almost every facet of village life has changed since then, from education, employment and recreational activities to transport, housing and the landscape. All these and other aspects have been affected by various changes to the economic infrastructure and revolutionary social and domestic advances. It is my hope that a representative flavour of those distant days has been captured within these pages for this generation, and others to follow, to read and enjoy.

Acknowledgements

For help and permission to use photographs and illustrations acknowledgment is made gratefully to many people but in particular to the friends, acquaintances and organisations given below:

The Hull Daily Mail Archive Library, The Yorkshire Post, Members of staff at the Local Studies Library, Hull, Local History and Reference Library, Beverley, East Riding of Yorkshire Council Archive Services, Beverley. Mr. Ernie Teal of the Sites and Monuments Records Office based at the Humberside Archeological Partnership building, Hull. Mr. Brian Crowther of the Hull and Barnsley Preservation Society. Gail Foreman of the Hull and East Riding Museum, High Street, Hull. Mr. Steve Goodhand of the Hull Transport Museum, Mr. Guy Jefferson, M.B.E. of the Yorkshire Air Museum Elvington Airfield, York, Innes Photographers, Hessle, Mr. Peter F. Lincoln, Mr. Ernie Coates, Mr. Alf W. Adamson, Mr. and Mrs. Norman V. Elliott, Mr. Edwin A.R. Trout, Mr. Peter Carver, Mrs. Jan Odey, Mr. Ray B. Warcup, Mrs. Marlene Thomas, Mr. Les Williamson, Mr. Otto Wegner, Mrs. Mollie Farthing, Mr. and Mrs. Douglas May, Mr. John Leonard, Mr. Geoff Hardwick, Mr. Ian Gibson, Mrs. Mollie Cutts, Mrs. Beryl Waddingham, Mrs. Gilbert Baitson, Mr. Michael Baitson, Mr. Mick Moverley, Mr. Fred W. Gratton, Patrica Gratton, Mrs. Jessie Holmes, Mrs. Anita May.

I also wish to extend my most sincere gratitude to Mr. and Mrs. Robert S. Bodenham for their time and patience in proof reading the draft of this book. My thanks are also due those listed below for their help with photographs and information:

Sue Adamson, Mrs. Sue Acey, Mrs. Mary Andrew, Mr. Fred Barlow, Mr. Frank E. Barratt, Mr. Jack Blacker, Dr. John Branch, Mr. and Mrs. Tony Brent, Captain Alan Brown, Mr. William Neville Brown, Marie E. Campbell, Mr. Bob Carr, Mr. Jim Carr, Mrs. Peggy Charlton, Mr. John Clutterbrook, Mrs. Edna Copeland, Mr. Phil Copeland, Mrs. Gladys Coxon, Mrs. Eve Crisp, Mr. Jack C. Crosby, Mrs. Louie Delgaty, Mrs. May Dennis, Mrs. Mary Dennis, Mrs. Edna Dobson, Mr. George Evison, Mr. Ronald Fairfax, Mr. Keith Fairly, Mrs. Anne Featherstone, Mr. and Mrs. Ken Fisher, Mr. Chris Foster, Mr. George Foster, Mr. Stephen Foster, Mr. Gerald Freeman, Mr. Geoff Grice, Mrs. Nellie Grisewood, Mr. David N. Haldenby, Mr. Alan Hall, Mr. and Mrs. Chris Hall, Mrs. Patty Hall, Mr. B. Harrison, Mrs. Victoria Herring, Mrs. Mary Hodgson, Mr. Carl Hogarth, Mr. Cecil Holtby, Mr. J. B. Holtby, Mr. Bruce Hornsey, Mrs. Ruby Hornsey, Mrs. Hannah Hotchin, Mrs. Pat Hotham, Mrs. Carole Howbridge, Mrs. Ruth Ireland, Mr. Anthony Jarman, Mr. and Mrs. Malcolm Jewitt, Mr. Norman Johnson, Mrs. Connie Lawson, Mr. Tim Lawson, Mr. R. D. Lucas, Betty Luke, Mrs. Mary Mason, Mrs. Cynthia May, Mr. and Mrs. Neil May, Mr. Lenny E. May, Mr. Malcolm C. Mews, Mr. and Mrs. Alan Moody, Mrs. Hilary Moore, Mrs. Rosalind Myers, Mr. Philip Needham, Mrs. Jackie Oxtoby, Mr. Geoff M. Percival, Mrs. Irene Renfrew, Mrs. Dorothy Roberts, Mrs. Pearl Scruton, Mrs. D. M. Shingles, Mrs. Betty Simpson, Marcia Smith, Mrs. Florence Skipsey, Mrs. Elsie Stone, Mr. Ben R. Taylor, Mrs. B. M. Thirsk, Mrs. Hazel Thornham, Mr. John Thornham, Mrs. Sandra Thornham, Mrs. Wendy Wales, Mrs. Bessie Walberton, Mr. John Waudby, Mr. Ian White, Mrs. Elsie Wiles, Mrs. M. V. Wilson, Mr. George W. Wilson, Mrs. Jannie M. Wolf, Mrs. Eileen Underwood.

Contents

Map of South Cave 1910

The Development of South Cave

The village of South Cave lies at the foot of the Yorkshire Wolds some 12 miles west of Hull and close to the A63 trunk road. The origins of its name are not certain and there remains considerable conjecture as to whether the name was derived from the Roman term for a hollow (cavus), or even perhaps from the French feudal barony of De Cave. The generally accepted view is that the names of both South Cave and its close neighbour North Cave were derived from the old English word 'caf' meaning swift or quick and refers to a stream, the water course being possibly the Mires Beck which flows from the Wolds through North Cave and which is joined by Cave Beck less than a mile from South Cave village.

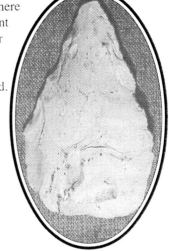

The settlement is believed to be Anglian, dating back to the 5th century A.D. although there is a great deal of evidence to suggest human habitation long before this period. A significant and fascinating find was made in October 1986 when an Acheulean hand-axe from the Lower Paleolithic Period (Old Stone Age), was discovered at Drewton which is situated about one and a half miles north east of South Cave. The pointed hand-axe is about 5 inches long and about 3 inches wide. Made from local stone the axe is believed to be about 200,000 years old.

The Acheulean hand-axe, seen right, found near Drewton by Mr. Stephen Foster was donated to the Hull and East Riding Museum, High Street, Hull. Hand-axes of this type were named after the village of St. Acheul in France where they were first found in large quantities about 150 years ago. The flint would have been shaped by holding the nodule firmly in one hand and a piece of bone would have been used to knock off small chips. Such axes were used for a variety of jobs - skinning animals, cutting up meat or digging up the roots of plants.

South Cave and its vicinity has also yielded a number of later finds from the Mesolithic and Bronze Age periods. At High Hunsley near Drewton two burial mounds were excavated during 1967-9 and proved to be round barrows of the Late Neolithic - Early Bronze Age period. In 1939 workmen quarrying for sand at Kettlethorpe, near South Cave discovered several human skeletons, together with an undamaged large and elaborately decorated food vessel made of well-baked clay which was estimated to be over 3,000 years old. Hull Museums Director Mr. Tom Sheppard was quoted at the time as saying the undamaged vessel was, *"One of the finest Bronze Age urns I have ever seen."* A further three Bronze Age burial mounds and pottery of the Beaker type were discovered in 1959 in the same sand quarry during an excavation by a York geologist and Hull museum staff.

This well-preserved rare Bronze Age food urn discovered at Kettlethorpe near South Cave in 1939, has the unusual feature of four feet, arranged crosswise and is decorated by two rows of impressions from twisted cords. Only six inches in height with a six inch diameter rim, the urn is remarkable for the elaborate extent to which it has been decorated over the entire surface from top to bottom. On the shoulder of the urn are four large bosses, perforated horizontally to take a cord for suspension.

Southern Britain was invaded by the Romans around 43 A.D. but it was not until 70 A.D. that northern Britain was conquered. A military base and fortress were constructed at Brough (named Petuaria by the Romans), on the northern bank of the River Humber. From the moorings at Brough Haven a road was constructed passing to the west of Elloughton to South Cave, diverging slightly to the east of the settlement through the field behind the present position of Ryeland House on Brough Road. It then passed through what are now known as Market Place and Station Road. A further turn in the road occurred at Kettlethorpe close to where the former South Cave railway station was later built, before diverging to the north along the route of the now modern road to South and North Newbald. Passing one mile west of Market Weighton, the Roman road joins the main road to York (Eboracum), via Stamford Bridge.

Numerous remains from the Roman period have been found in the area such as brooches, coins and pottery. At the corner of Market Place and Beverley Road some fragments of Roman vases and a portion of pavement were dug up in the late 19th century. In December 1913 the Brough Gas Company, while laying gas pipes in the same area, reported finding other portions of tessellated pavement. Much later excavations in 1994 carried out by the Humberside Archaeology Unit during the construction of an extension to a residential property near East Lodge in Station Road, also revealed a significant amount of pottery sherds further suggesting the existence of a Romano-British settlement in South Cave.

One of the most exciting chance Roman finds was made in January 1890 by a farmer called Joseph Pinder, while ploughing an area known as 'The Cliffs' or slopes of Mount Airy. Mr. Pinder discovered a pig of solid lead, buried vertically and only slightly below the surface. On later examination it was found to measure 22 inches in length, 5 inches in breadth, 4 inches in

depth, and weighed 9st 9lb. Along one side an inscription reads, "C. IVL. PROTI. BRIT. LVT. EX. ARG." This may be expanded to read, *"Caii Iulii Proti Britannicum Lutudense ex argento"* and translates as, "C. Julius Protus, British (lead) from Lutudae." C. Julius Protus was the superintendent or lessee of the Lutudae mine in Matlock, South Derbyshire where the block was smelted.

Seven other lead pigs have been found this century in the district and all were discovered near the River Humber. Following the discovery of the South Cave pig of lead Mr. C.E G. Barnard the owner of the land paid Mr. Pinder a sum of £5 and had it removed to his residence at Cave Castle, much to the disappointment of those who wished to see it placed for general public display. It was not until 1925 when the contents of Cave Castle were sold by the trustees of the Barnard family estate, that it was finally presented to the Municipal Museum in Albion Street, Hull.

The Romans were followed by the Anglo-Saxons and later the Danes, who destroyed many signs of the Roman occupation in the area but left behind them evidence of their own settlements. An Anglo-Saxon cemetery was discovered at nearby Everthorpe in 1958 during the construction of new building work at H.M. Prison, Everthorpe.

Place names such as Kettlethorpe, (Chetel's Torp), Everthorpe, (Yvers Torp), Riplingham, Brantingham, Broomfleet, (fleet - a stream), Faxfleet, Yokefleet, Drewton, Elloughton, Weedley are all derived from the Anglo-Saxon and Danish periods of occupation. Gamel, an Anglo-Saxon was the first recorded Lord of the Manor for the South Cave area. Later, at the time of the Domesday Survey in 1083 (which was produced for taxation purposes for King William I and culminated in the Domesday Book of 1086), the Manor of Cave was held by Robert Malet, son of William Malet of Normandy and was described as a community consisting of about 30 villeins, with two water mills, a church and a priest. By the 13th century, the large Domesday estate belonging to Robert Malet had been divided up into three manors. The principal manor was known as the Bailiwick or Manor Paramount with East Hall. The other estates were known as West Hall Manor and Faxfleet.

It is thought that the church referred to in the 11th century was most likely to have been a wooden construction which would have stood in the same position as the present church of All Saints' situated near the western end of the village. However, no vestiges of the original church have survived nor of the houses used by the villeins clustered around it. Later, in the early Middle Ages the settlement began to develop to the east of the church at the point where the road from Hull to the West Riding crosses the old Roman road leading from Brough to York. Because of these route connections this site was obviously a natural trading centre, a crossroads where two agricultural regions met and so it is hardly surprising that a market evolved.

The earliest reference to a market at Cave is dated 1156. This was over a century before the granting of a charter in 1291 by King Edward I to the Master and Brethren of the Knights Templars in England and their successors for a market on Monday in every week at their Manor in South Kave (sic) and, *"One fair there every year for four days, namely on the eve, day and morrow of the Holy Trinity and one day following."* By this charter South Cave became a "town" but never achieved "borough" status. Other charters in the 14th and 15th centuries confirmed the earlier grant.

In the 12th century the village was known as 'Maracave' and 'Marchedcave' indicating the holding of a market there and by the 13th century the prefix was used to distinguish South Cave from its close neighbour to the north. By the late 18th century, as a result of agricultural improvements South Cave became a thriving corn trading centre, with corn being shipped via the River Humber to Hull and Howdendyke as well as to Leeds, Wakefield and other West Riding towns. This trade resulted in the building of the Market Hall in 1796 where much corn was traded. Indeed, the metal hooks in the ceiling on which corn was hung are still visible today in the portico entrance of the hall. The introduction of the railways in the 1840s giving easier and quicker access to larger markets resulted in the gradual decline in the corn trade. The market survived until the mid 19th century, and the fair up to the outbreak of the Second World War.

Since the late 18th century the village of South Cave has been uniquely divided by the grounds of the Barnard family's Gothic house Cave Castle which is now a hotel, restaurant and golf club. Up until this time, the properties in the North and South Cave area were built of oolite limestone which was quarried locally. Following the opening of the Newport brickworks in the 1780s the use of oolite limestone rapidly declined and the quarries gradually fell into disuse becoming overgrown or used as refuse tips. The limestone occurs in thick beds varying from 20 to 30 feet in depth and dates from the Middle Jurassic period, being predominately cream and blue-gray coloured. It can still be seen in the walls of some of the older cottages in the area. On the weathered surfaces can be seen the characteristic "oolitic" structures (small round or oval concretions of lime), called "oolites" which resemble the eggs of fish. One of the best locations for examining Cave oolite is the old Eastfield Quarry just

Above, local farmer and retired geology teacher John Waudby with assistant John Leonard examining a broken 'dogger' in the South Cave Station Quarry. The Kellaways sands and limestone are well exposed here but it is within the boulder-like stones known as 'doggers' that fossils are found. They are exceedingly hard and dense and it is only with great difficulty that they can be broken. Nevertheless, Mr. Waudby has found a number of interesting fossils including this large ammonite held by Mr. Leonard. The ammonite is dated to approximately 170 million years old and its shell would have once been the home of a small octopus type sea creature. Above left, a drawing of a Plesiosaur. The bones of a large dinosaur of this type were found at nearby Elloughton where the same Kellaways series is present.

south of the former South Cave railway station. Interestingly, oolite limestone from this particular quarry was extensively used in the construction of Beverley Minster in the 11th century.

The similarly disused Station Quarry site (opposite the former Eastfield Quarry) and the neighbouring area are also known for the Kellaways series of soft sands and hard sandstone. The Station Quarry site has revealed a rich variety and abundance of fossils. Geologists have excavated here for more than a century. During the late 1890s the skeletal remains of a huge saurian (or lizard like dinosaur), dating from about 150 million years ago, were discovered by Tom Sheppard, protruding from an exposed quarry face at Mill Hill at nearby Elloughton. Specimens of the skeleton were examined by a paleontologist and the bones were reported to have originated from an animal allied to the Plesiosaur, a carnivorous marine reptile around 36 feet long which had a long neck and paddle-like limbs. This prehistoric creature dates from the Jurassic period when most of Britain and Northern Europe were covered by shallow seas. The remains were taken to the Municipal Museum, Hull but were thought to have been lost during the bombing raids on the city during the Second World War.

The parish once included the now depopulated hamlet of Weedley, the village of Broomfleet situated along the banks of the River Humber and the small hamlet of Faxfleet. Weedley, on the high ground at the eastern part of the parish of South Cave, had the distinction in 1185 of having the earliest recorded existence of a windmill in England. The hamlet is thought to have disappeared by the 14th century. Each of the three later became separate civil parishes for local government purposes.

For many centuries agriculture followed the open field system until the Enclosure Act was completed in 1787, when the practice of having the land divided into strips and held in common by the inhabitants was changed to one of large hedged fields. Local land enclosures were following in the wake of the national trend resulting in the ability to provide much larger crops. Agriculture is still very important to the local economy, although increasingly during the last quarter of the 20th century more and more farmland has been and continues to be used for housing development. As a result South Cave is becoming a large residential village and along with other neighbouring villages, part of the West Hull suburban complex.

Although technically classed as a market town complete with Town Hall, it is considered by many to have more of the features of a village, such as the existence of only a few small shops and a population figure of around 3,300 people. At the present time, residential development continues apace adding to the concerns of the South Cave Parish Council by exacerbating the already serious problems of traffic.

The older parts of the village were designated as a conservation area by the Humberside County Council in 1974. In essence, a conservation area is an area of special architectural or historic interest whose character or appearance should be preserved or enhanced and in these areas planning controls are more strict. While conservation controls have certainly been effective in the village, it is hoped that under an important new initiative by the parish council, residents will be encouraged to support a Village Design Statement which basically specifies what are the qualities and attributes of a village. Once the document is drawn up it is likely to be formally accepted as a part of the planning guidelines for the area and any future development or alterations to South Cave will have to abide by that guidance.

Brough Road

Right, the road leading into the Market Place from Brough Road. It was known as Humber Street in the 17th and 18th centuries. In the 1930s a single carriageway bypass was built south of the village. This was later improved into a dual carriageway and in 1972 a new elaborate junction with the South Cave-Market Weighton road was constructed as part of other roadworks between Welton and North Cave.

Ryeland Hill

In the early 1770s, a Scotsman named George McTurk (1750-1845), from Cumnock in Ayrshire came with his brother James (1748-1829) to the East Riding to help with the building of the Market Weighton Canal. They both made their initial wealth during their employment on this project and they settled in New Village, (the southern part of Newport), which had been developed following the draining of Wallingfen.

James opened the first public house in Newport known as the Turk's Head in 1777. Meanwhile, George married Ann Grasby of South Cave in March 1788 and became a tenant farmer in the village, farming first at Mount Airy and later at West End.

One of their ten children, Thomas (1793-1857), altered the spelling of his surname to MacTurk and subsequently became established as a well known woollen merchant, Thomas MacTurk and Co., of Hull. His warehouse was situated on South Church Side, in the Market Place, Hull.

Upon Thomas's death his son George Gladstone MacTurk, (1831-1911), returned to South Cave from Bradford where he had been practising as a solicitor to takeover his father's woollen business and the large rambling property of Ryeland Hill which

had been built a few years earlier for his father. The house was ideal for George and his wife Ellen who had a large family of 11 children.

In addition to continuing the family's business George set himself up as a solicitor in South Cave and became Chairman of the South Cave and Wallingfen Local Board, promoting a scheme for road improvements.

In 1872 he provided the village with one of the first piped water supplies in the district, based on springs to the east of the village. This new water supply replaced the old water pumps which had been erected in 1854 by parish officers.

After his death in 1911, Ryeland Hill, along with a number of other properties he owned including the Fox and Coney public-house and 158 acres of land in and around South Cave were publicly auctioned in the Church Institute in Church Street.

The house has had a succession of owners and in 1987 a planning appeal to turn Ryeland Hill into a £1 million-plus leisure complex by a Hull restaurant owner was refused. Today the property has been converted into a small number of luxury flats.

Ryeland Hill

Netherwolds, built in the 1890s for Annie (one of George MacTurk's granddaughters) and her husband the Reverend Joshua Wimbush of Finchley. The name Netherwolds translates as "Beneath the Wolds."

The Gallows

To the north eastern side of Brough Road was a field formerly known as Gallows Flatt or Whitley Pitt Close which is where the village gallows once stood. In 1275 the Knights Templars as Lords of the Manor were recorded as claiming ownership of them.

In the Middle Ages every town, abbey and the manorial lords had the right of hanging and gallows were repulsive but familiar features of the English countryside erected in conspicuous positions where they could be seen by all. The offender died in the sunshine or under grey skies and in the presence of a crowd which would probably include his family and friends.

Hanging was often used as a punishment even for minor offences. It was not until the Consolidation Act, passed in 1861 that hanging was confined to treason and wilful murder. It is known that, in South Cave, hangings had ceased by the end of the 17th century. In 1703 a Henry Mounder of South Cave murdered his brother but was tried at York Assizes and executed by hanging at the city's castle.

During the medieval period a very similar gallows to this one stood on Brough Road, south of the Market Place.

Bacchus Lane

The lane is shown as Bakehouse Lane on an 1855 survey map, but this is thought to have been an error, since there never was a bakehouse situated there. Its correct name is Bacchus Lane named in recognition of the family of William and Ann Bacchus who resided there as far back as the 16th century. The lane formerly ran from Market Place to Water Lane at West End, but part of it was blocked off in the late 18th century after the parkland of the Castle was extended into bull pasture.

The King George V Memorial Playing Field in Bacchus Lane was donated to the village by Mr. James Wright Carmichael of Cave Castle on Saturday, 5th August 1939. On that same day the official opening ceremony took place in the presence of a large crowd of local people and just before Mr. Carmichael's speech the band of the 433 Battery 61st (South Lancashire), Searchlight Regiment R.A. (T.A.), sounded a fanfare of trumpets. The ceremony was followed by a children's fancy dress parade, a maypole dance, various stalls and sports. In 1950 a recreation ground in nearby Church Street was acquired by a specially formed trust. A children's play area was later integrated with the playing field and a community sports centre was built near the recreation ground in 1978.

Hall's Poultry Farm which once stood on the west side of Brough Road near Bacchus Lane. The business was started by Patty and her husband Arthur Hall and continued for about 25 years until the site was sold for housing development in the late 1970s. There were 5 sheds (originally army barrack huts), containing 6,000 chickens producing fertile eggs which were sent to Ripon to be hatched and reared into broiler chickens. Patty had come to live in South Cave in 1921 when she was 13 years old with her three brothers and six sisters. Her father Josiah Moate took on the tenancy of Market Place Farm, which had been let previously to the Pinder family by the Cave Castle estate. Following the sale of the estate in 1939 the farm was bought by Rob Wilson. Patty is seen here feeding some of her chickens.

Market Place

The Market Place was once known as Hemp Garth. It is a long broad road, having a natural slope from both north and south ends of the village. Looking down to the left of the photograph taken c.1907 can be seen the corner of Church Street, (formerly called West Street). This road leads down to the western end of the village. On the right is the junction with Beverley Road while the road leading through the Market Place is part of the old Roman road from Lincoln to York. In the 17th century bull baiting took place in the Market Place. From Elizabethan times such practice was the national custom before bulls could be presented for sale and consumption. This usually meant tying a bull to a stake and setting dogs upon it. This cruel act was supposed to make the meat more tender and fines were imposed if the animals were killed without baiting. The ritual was finally outlawed by Parliament during in the 19th century.

Taken from the Town Hall tower, a turn of the century view looking up towards Brough Road. On the right of the picture can be seen the old Three Tuns public house and next door Mr. W. A. Suddaby's grocery shop. The last cottage on the left-hand side on the brow of the hill still stands today and is one of the oldest surviving properties in the village. An early to mid 18th century building it is a single storey dwelling built of local oolitic limestone. A number of houses in the village date from the mid to late 18th and early 19th centuries. The larger examples include those at numbers 22 and 30 Market Place.

Left, Rawdale's Farm, Market Place in 1939. At the turn of the century there were 27 farmers in South Cave, numerous market gardeners and small-holders. Although several farms have since gone, agriculture is still an important part of village life. During the 1960s land at Rawdale's Farm was sold for housing development. The farmhouse is now a private residence.

Right, farm labourers taking a well earned tea-break during threshing time at Rawdale's Farm c.1910. The Watson family of Brantingham were the threshing machine contractors for the area taking their sets from farm to farm when required.

Town Hall

South Cave's focal point is the Town Hall, now a Grade II listed building. During the 18th century South Cave had a prosperous corn trade which resulted in the erection of a Town Hall in 1796 in the Market Place. The two-storeyed building with a turret and cupola above a pediment was designed by Henry Boldero Barnard on the site of the old market cross. The building originally served as a market hall with a schoolroom for the village children. It consisted of an open arcade facing the street where corn was bought and weighed, a ground floor area for the sale of diary produce, a schoolroom above and a house behind for the schoolmaster. The Jubilee clock tower was added in 1887 to commemorate Queen Victoria's Golden Jubilee at a cost of £120. The Hull News reported on Tuesday the 21st June, *"The clock was formally set in motion by Mrs. Barnard of Cave Castle. As the clock struck twelve, three ringing cheers were given for the Queen by the vast assembly ..."* In 1935 to commemorate the Silver Jubilee of King George V and Queen Mary the clock tower was illuminated by public subscription.

In former times proclamations were made on the steps of the building. The hiring of labour occurred there too. Here are members of the South Cave Subscription Silver Band heralding the announcement of the crowning of King George VI in May 1937. South Cave, in times past, employed a town crier whose duties would include standing on the Town Hall steps ringing the market-bell at the opening and closing of the market. The bellringer also walked around the village stopping every 100 yards or so to announce items of news. He was an important figure in the days when many people could not read and newspapers were scarce. In 1938 the post of parish bellringer became vacant following the resignation of Harry Waudby who had held the position for a number of years. Frank Jude was subsequently appointed at 3 shillings per ringing session. However, his services had been dispensed with by early September 1939, upon the outbreak of the Second World War when a nationwide ban came into force prohibiting any type of bell ringing except to warn of enemy invasion.

The Cross School

From 1700 a schoolmaster taught lessons from a room in a small cottage owned by the parish in the West End of the village. But, as the numbers of pupils increased, the room became progressively inadequate.

Following the Enclosures Award of 1787 the parish was granted some 10 acres of land in lieu of common rights. A site was found in the Market Place and with the help of public subscriptions a market hall, with a schoolroom on its first floor, and a master's house behind, was completed by 1796.

Known as the Cross School it was at first supported by subscriptions and school pence. By 1817 it had become an established Church School united with the National Society. It is believed that up until c.1843 it was a mixed school.

On Saturday, 14th January 1804 an advertisement was placed in the Hull Advertiser for a new schoolmaster and schoolmistress. Robert Sharp and his wife Ann from Bridlington were the successful applicants and took up their posts shortly afterwards with a joint annual salary of fifty guineas.

Robert Sharp kept a diary of village life from 1812 to 1837. This diary mainly in the form of letters, addressed to his son William who worked in London for a publishing company, gives a unique and fascinating insight into life in South Cave between the Napoleonic Wars and the early Victorian era. It was eventually bound into one volume and c.1972 presented to the County Record Office by Robert Sharp's great, great granddaughter Miss Florence Jane Dennis.

As one of the most educated men in South Cave, he became involved in many roles such as village constable, tax collector, land surveyor and general local advisor on legal matters. He remained Master of the Cross School until his death on the 5th May 1843, aged 69 years. William Thomas Bruce who was born at Grantham in Lincolnshire in 1816 came to South Cave about 1843 as a successor to Robert Sharp as the new Master of the school, a post he retained until about 1872.

For just over 39 years Robert Sharp had educated several generations of local children and had played an active part in village affairs. His obituary placed in the Hull Advertiser on the 12th May 1843 read, *"Much and deservedly respected by all who knew him."* Following her husband's death Ann Sharp is believed to have moved to Church Street, South Cave, where she was living with her granddaughter Ann Condor in 1851. Ann Sharp died in 1868 aged 92 years.

By 1893 conditions in the school had deteriorated so much that the infants classroom was condemned. Two years later the Cross School over the market hall was closed and at a cost of £600 a new boys school was built on a site south of Rawdale Farm provided by Charles E.G.B. Barnard. The new school was opened on the 6th March 1895 and was administered by a committee of managers, the headmaster being a Mr. James Johnson.

In 1899 the Reverend T. J. Miller, Chairman of the School Managers had a disagreement with Mr. George Moverley, who represented the parents on the committee. He removed Mr. Moverley from office and as a result many parents curtailed their subscriptions whereupon the vicar withdrew all church funding and closed the school.

Soon it was reopened with the appointment of a new teacher, Mr. Dennis, in charge. Even so, only four pupils attended, the remaining seventy nine having returned to the old Cross School with Mr. Johnson, supported by the National Union

South Cave Parish Council formed in 1894, took over the Cross Building in 1903. The first meeting of the Parish Council (after the alterations were completed) was held on Tuesday, 18th September 1906. The building subsequently became known as the Town Hall and is now a Grade II listed building. Today, as well as the Parish Council chamber the Town Hall houses the offices of Ray Rackham's accountancy business. A flag pole costing £650 was purchased by the Parish Council for the Town Hall and to commemorate the event a special flag raising ceremony was held on Sunday, 1st March 1998 which was witnessed by a crowd of local onlookers.

WANTED IMMEDIATELY, a MASTER and MISTRESS, for the MARKET-CROSS School, at South-Cave; they must be of good moral Character, and able to produce satisfactory proof thereof.

Applications by letter, post-paid, to Mr. John Levitt, Ellerker; or to Mr. Witty, the present Teacher, South Cave. will meet due attention.

Above, the 1804 advertisement for a new schoolmaster, to which Robert Sharp and his wife Ann successfully replied.

of Teachers who paid his salary.

It was reported by the newspapers of the day that the scene in the village was lively, the vicar and Mr. Dennis having to be escorted to the reopening of the school by a policeman amid, *"groans and hoots"* from the assembled crowd. Mr. Johnson, conversely received an ovation, being greeted with banners and cheers.

The argument quickly escalated into a legal battle over the management and ownership of the two school buildings. Mrs. Sophia Barnard and the villagers brought an action against the vicar and churchwardens which was finally settled out of court in her favour.

Mrs. Barnard took possession of the school, paid off the mortgage of £250 and re-instated the managers, leasing the premises to them at a nominal fee of one shilling per annum.

On the 7th January 1901 James Johnson returned to school after an absence of 22 months and readmitted the four boys who had attended the vicar's school. The Boys' School together with the Girls' School in Church Street were closed in 1967 when the present mixed school was opened in the same year.

The schoolroom above the old market hall where Robert Sharp would have taught his pupils the principles of reading, writing and arithmetic. In 1906 some time after the final closure of the schoolroom a Parish Council Chamber was opened following considerable alterations and improvements to the building.

Below, the schoolmaster's house at the back of the Town Hall where Robert Sharp lived from 1804-1843 and wrote his diaries. Only a small area of the original garden remains as over many years plots were sold for building purposes.

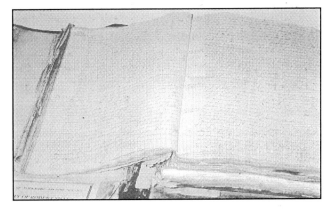

Above, present at the book launch was the great-great grandson of Robert Sharp, Mr. William Neville Brown with his young grandson Edward Thomas Brown. William expressed his delight at the transcription and publication of the diaries. He attended the second Boys' School (built in 1895), from 1935-1945 leaving school at the age of 14 years. He took up employment as a drawing office boy at the Blackburn Aircraft Factory in Brough and worked there for 47 years before finally retiring as a Principal Design Engineer in 1992.

By courtesy of the East Riding of Yorkshire Council Archive Services, Robert Sharp's original manuscript volume containing his diary and letters were placed on display at South Cave Town Hall in November 1997. This was to celebrate the launch of a 700 page book entitled "The Diary of Robert Sharp of South Cave: Life in a Yorkshire Village 1812-1837." Transcribed and researched by Cottingham academics Janice and Peter Crowther, the book took almost five years to complete.

This photograph taken in June 1909 shows some of the pupils from the Boys' School with the Headmaster, Mr. Percy Woodford and infants teacher Miss Maud Wells. From the top row left to right, Leslie Wallgate, Allan Moverley, Edward Fewster, William Brinkley, Walter Cockin, Arthur Underwood, Reginald Smith, Harry Underwood. From the middle row left to right, Albert Dennis, Walter Young, Colin Mason, Fred Atkinson, Jack Wilson, Walter Donkin, Ernest Laverick, Arthur Davis, Ernest Wiles. Bottom row left to right, George Freeman, Albert Burley, Joseph Thornham, William Cockin, Robert Alcock, Frank Waudby Jnr., Frank Warcup, Arthur Stather, Walter Gibson, Robert Burley,

Stocks and Pillory

The Statute of Labourers (1350), enjoined every town to provide stocks, between the passing of the Act and the Pentecost of that year. A further Act was passed in 1405 to include the provision of stocks in every village.

Frequently, as in South Cave, the stocks were combined with a wooden pillory and whipping post similar to the one shown in the drawing on the right. It will be observed that they were designed to hold up to four delinquents, namely, one in the pillory, one at the whipping post and two in the stocks.

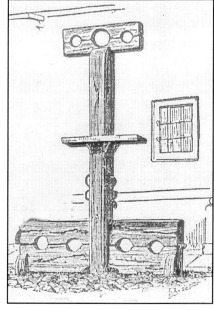

The custom was to place the offender(s) in this contraption during the opening times of a market and the public would be invited to pelt them with rotten fruit and eggs.

Bench Book 4, folio 226, *b* from the Kingston upon Hull Corporation Records and dated 1581-2, states that on 11th January a widow named Jane Smythe, "*... did curse Mr. Mair, the justices, his brethren, and the preacher, speakinge false and slanderous wordes against them ...*"

Subsequently, Jane Smythe publicly announced that, "*... she wished and trusted to see as great plague to come to the towne as ever their was.*" For her impertinence and rudeness to the town officials it was decreed that she should be taken the next day and set in the stocks in the Market Place with a paper on her head describing her offence.

Robert Marshall, who was Town Constable in 1821 is recorded as having the responsibility to ensure the repair of the instruments of punishment. He obtained from George Petfield the local joiner, a pair of stocks and two oak posts, the latter evidently for the pillory, for the sum of £1. 14s. 0d.

In line with many other civil and legal reforms of the 1830s the use of the pillory was abolished by statute in 1837. The use of the stocks however, was never officially abolished and for many years the idea that both the stocks and pillory should be used in lieu of committal to prison lasted long after prisons had become more generally available. The actual date when the stocks and pillory were last used in South Cave is unknown. It is believed that they were removed sometime before 1870 from their site near the Three Tuns public house which formerly stood on the corner of Church Street and Market Place.

Dated Monday, 10th June 1912, this pair of photographs taken at the junction of Church Street and Market Place shows onlookers viewing the extent of the flooding caused by a thunderstorm. It is recalled that dead rats and other rubbish came floating across the Market Place and down Church Street. Over a period of two weeks chalk and flint were washed down from the hill tops and down Beverley Road to a depth of two feet completely blocking the road. All the local market gardeners used their horses and carts to help remove the debris. Although a notable event, it was by no means an isolated incident. Early records show that during Cave Fair in 1841, lightening struck in the vicinity of Mount Airy during the course of another violent thunderstorm. Constant driving rain caused great rivers of water and vegetation to descend the hills which consequently flooded the village. The stalls in the Market Place were swept away and the cellars of the houses were engulfed with water. The most destructive flood on record for South Cave occurred in June 1883 when thousands of tons of chalk rubble were again washed down from the hill tops into the north eastern area of the village. The beck was full of rubble for more than a mile and some of the rocks and boulders were carried as far as the River Humber. Flooding also caused great damage to the Hull and Barnsley West Junction Railway which was then under construction. In 1889, again the village was flooded and it is reported that villagers had to cross the Market Place in makeshift boats. A freak thunderstorm in June 1950 was reported to have again turned the streets into temporary rivers. However, better drainage, the planting of hedgerows and the continuous planting of woodland on the surrounding steep hill sides have played a great part in protecting the relevant areas from denudation and have prevented subsequent flooding.

Left, a late 19th century view of the beck bridge taken from inside the Three Tuns public house which once stood at the junction of Church Street and Market Place. It is documented that on occasions chloride of lime was added to the beck water to prevent smells and disease. One of the old 18th century local by-laws decreed that, "... no person corrupt the Town Beck by letting into it stinking or hurtful water or washing unwholesome things in the same ..." This beck bridge and a length of the beck running along Church Street were covered over in the early 1960s, in order to widen the thoroughfare for traffic.

Right, in pre-war years John Warcup used to sweep out the open beck for three shillings per week. He requested an extra sixpence per week which was granted but to his annoyance he was given the additional task of winding up the Town Hall clock. John as a young man took an apprenticeship with a veterinary surgeon but never finished it due to a lack of financial support. Nevertheless, he was looked upon as the unofficial village vet-cum-doctor for those who could not afford to pay for such services. It was said that he could cure either animal or human ailments with his many concoctions of powders and medicines that he made up and dispensed.

Shops and Trades People

A great many shops and businesses have come and gone over the centuries in South Cave, especially around the old Market Place area. Up until the widespread use of public transport and private car ownership the village was a self-sufficient community with its own market and virtually every service and need could be catered for.

In the mid to late 19th century as well as numerous farmers and market gardeners there were upwards of fifty tradesmen and craftsmen in the village, ranging from Thomas Vause's blacksmiths shop, William Gibson's wheelwright and joiners shop, Petfield & Farthing's iron-founders and implement makers, William Cousens plumber and glaziers, Thomas Kemp, tinman and brazier, Thomas Goodwill, bricklayers, Thornham's shoemakers business, John Waudby tailor and grocer, Thomas Leake, butcher and Henry Anderson who traded as a grocer but also offered a hairdressing service.

As far back as 1668 we can see that South Cave as a market town must have been a place of considerable importance, since one of its shopkeepers a John Chapilow was able to issue his own halfpenny-token as a means of currency.

The Post Office

Before the introduction of mail coaches in the 18th century Britain's mail was carried from town to town by horse riders known as post boys. They would stop at the post-houses (usually inns), to collect and deliver mail. As the mail coaches and then the railways and roads spread throughout the country, the use of post boys diminished.

Already a well established market town, South Cave had the only post office between Howden and Hull on the newly arranged post road connecting the Great North Road at Doncaster through to Hull. William Goodlad was the local postmaster as well as the innkeeper at the Fox and Coney for some years before his death in 1789.

For many years the post road passed through Everthorpe, up Swinescaife near Drewton and through Riplingham, as may be seen on Geldart's Map of 1799 printed in J. G. Hall's, *History of South Cave, 1892.*

The post road from Market Weighton to South Cave passed through Newbald and crossed the post road from Doncaster to Hull at the corner of Everthorpe Lane. Mail would be exchanged at this point. From the South Cave Parish Registers are the following entries:-

"Henry Stephenson, from York, Horse rider, buried June 29, 1740."

Henry was probably the horse post messenger on the York-South Cave route as were the following,

"Frances Hall, a post boy, thrown from his horse, buried Nov. 30, 1756."

" William, son of William Johnson, horse rider, buried Feb. 18, 1779."

The introduction in January 1840 of the prepaid penny postage stamp for any distance within the United Kingdom led to a massive increase in its use and many new post offices throughout the country were opened.

North Cave was operating a post office by 1857 and the village of Hotham had its own post office by 1872. Even the nearby hamlet of Everthorpe had its own post office by 1875.

Mr. George Chapman is recorded as South Cave Postmaster in 1892, the Market Place Office being described as the *"Post, Money Order, Telegraph, Savings Bank, Insurance and Annuity Office."* Following Mr. Chapman's death in 1896 his wife Mary ran the business. Following Mary's death in 1905 Mr. Walter Waudby became the sub-postmaster.

By 1929, in addition to all the services then on offer Mr. Waudby was also enlisted as the local Registrar of Births and Deaths. In 1914 the Post Office moved from No. 55, to new premises at No. 75, Market Place and in the 1950s to 27 Church Street. Finally, it moved to its present site at No. 24, Market Place.

Only four specimens of the above halfpenny token (not to size) issued by John Chapilow in 1668 are known to exist. Following the restoration of the monarchy in 1660 there was a serious shortage of copper and a series of tokens were issued by tradesmen and others to overcome the problem. However, they eventually became a nuisance as there were so many different types.

HER MAJESTY'S ROYAL MAIL from Hull to Doncaster, *via* Cave, Howden, Booth-Ferry, and Thorne, will commence RUNNING on THURSDAY, the 6th July, from the Cross-Keys Hotel, Market-Place, Hull; every Morning at a Quarter before FIVE o'Clock; and from the New Angel Doncaster, every Afternoon, at TWO o'Clock, *and not at Five in the Morning as before advertised.*

Passengers and Parcels booked at the Cross-Keys, Market-Place, Hull; Half Moon, Howden; Red Lion and White Hart, Thorne; and New Angel Doncaster—for Sheffield or Doncaster.

The Sheffield Coach leaves Doncaster Half-an-Hour after the arrival of the Mail.

THOS. GELDARD and CO., Hull.
WELLS, HUDSON, & CO., Booth-Ferry.
GEO. DUNHILL and CO., Doncaster.

Above, mail coaches first ran in 1784 and carried letters as well as passengers. Featured above, is an advertisement which appeared in the Hull Packet dated Thursday, 29th June 1837 announcing a change in the time of departure of the royal mail coach which travelled through South and North Cave on its way to Doncaster.

Above, standing in the doorway of the Market Place Post Office is Sub-Postmaster Walter Waudby, (1868-1944), who also operated a joinery business from the premises. Top left, an earlier photograph taken of Mr. Waudby's post office and staff c.1907. By 1914, Walter had moved the business further up Market Place vacating the old premises for Emma Butterfield who opened them as a confectionery shop and who was there until she retired c.1945. Next door was John Waudby's tailor shop and farmstead. In the window there was a tailor's goose, a wide platform where the tailor sat cross-legged to sew. John Waudby's family had been tailors for generations. Prior to being a tailors shop it was a public house. Originally, the pub which ceased trading c.1858 had been known as the Blacksmith's Arms (est. 1825), before being renamed the Prince Albert c.1840. Today, the premises are occupied by a Chinese Take Away and Fried Fish Shop.

Above, Henry Anderson and family outside his Market Place shop, c.1890. Ray Warcup recalls that when he was a child in the 1930s, two Anderson sisters Rebecca and Ada ran the shop. "We used to buy gobstoppers there, a farthing each or four for a penny. It took almost an hour to suck one, they would change colour as you sucked them and they were as big as golf balls." Below, during the 1940s Anderson's shop was taken over by Francis Myers Ltd., who also had premises in Welton.

Norman Calvert drove the first Co-op van which was a small three wheeled vehicle and used to take deliveries around the South Cave area. He is seen here c.1937 with Gerald Freeman at the wheel. Following the Second World War Norman went into business as a wet fish merchant, delivering around the district in his distinctive van, upon which was painted a large mermaid. Norman was affectionately known as "Coddy" Calvert. In 1963 Norman and his wife Olive sold the business and moved to Broomfleet Post Office.

Above right, the Co-operative store which formerly stood on the corner of Church Street, Market Place.

Freeman's Painting and Decorating business was established c.1904 and operated from No.64, Market Place. James Frederick Freeman the proprietor is seen here complete with overalls, standing outside some cottages with George Donkin, carrier and cart owner, near the old Congregational Church at West End.

Walter Henry Scott was born in North Cave and was brother to Anthony Eland Scott who ran a grocery shop there. Walter's first chemist and drapery shop was in Witham, Hull. He transferred his business to South Cave in c.1903 and opened his new shop premises at number 81, Market Place (above). Older villagers remember the custom of the annual scramble, when on New Year's Day children would gather around local shops shouting "Hip, hip, hooray" until the shopkeepers appeared in the doorway with baskets of sweets, nuts, coins or fruit. Walter would often appear with hot pennies in a bucket which he would throw out onto the road for the children to chase after.

Following Walter Scott's retirement c.1929 his shop became Ward's Grocery Stores until 1933 when L. B Walker took over this business. Following numerous owners through the years it is now a newsagents shop.

Far right, Challenger Alcock, M.R.C.V.S veterinary surgeon in South Cave between 1876-c.1922. He was originally from Ulceby in Lincolnshire and served an apprenticeship at the veterinary firm of Marshall & Wragg of London. At the conclusion of his training he moved to Pocklington in East Yorkshire where he practiced as a vet for a short time before moving to South Cave with his widowed mother Sarah. In October 1876 Challenger commenced his own veterinary practice at number 50, Market Place. Among his list of clients were Lord Muncaster of Warter Hall, Pocklington, Colonel Clitherow of Hotham Hall, Major Carver of North Cave and Christopher Sykes M.P. of Brantingham Hall. Challenger Alcock retired from his long running practice c.1922. In 1909 Challenger and his wife Marie opened tea-rooms in the same building as the surgery but this particular business venture was not a success. Later, during the 1920s Marie opened a fried fish and chip shop on the premises which was taken over by their daughter Mabel in 1940. Robert Edmund Alcock, (1901-1969), youngest of five children and their only son started an electrical business behind the shop and later in 1937 built a house and electrical shop in the Market Place which he ran with his wife Ethel. Robert known as Bob was quite an entrepreneur operating the first motor-taxi business as well as the first electric cinema in the village.

Right, Bob Alcock in 1958 with his latest taxi, a Standard Triumph.

In 1969 Bob's widow Ethel sold the shop and house at No. 63, Market Place to Mr. Malcolm Mews who continued an electrical business there until his retirement in 1995. Left, this photograph was taken during the conversion of the shop frontage into a private house for Mr. Mews in the same year. Here we see the original shop sign which was discovered following the removal of Mr. Mews' sign. Bob's daughter Marlene Thomas is seen here standing in the doorway of the former family property.

Above, Fred and Florrie Grattons newsagency and grocery shop at number 32, Market Place. The Grattons took the premises over in about 1957 from W. H. and E. Scutt, who sold groceries and drapery. Mr. and Mrs. Scutt, however, still continued to live in the house attached to the shop until their deaths in 1971. Above right, the well stocked interior of Grattons Market Place shop. In 1962 the Grattons sold the business to a Mr. Davies who because of financial difficulties closed it early in 1965. Mr. and Mrs. Alan Moody from Hull bought the empty shop in August of that year.

Open Sunday   Telephone N. Cave 629

A. MOODY

32 MARKET PLACE, SOUTH CAVE

Sweets and Tobacco   Frozen Foods   Ice Cream

Bread and Confectionery Fresh Daily

Greeting Cards for all Occasions   Paper-backs and Childrens Books

Fruit and Vegetables

In 1973 Rosalind and Gordon Myers bought the business at number 32, Market Place from Mr. Alan Moody and also purchased the house from a Mr. Tomlinson who had inherited it from Mr. and Mrs. Scutt. Following 25 years of ownership by the Myers, their shop known as Centre Stores finally closed on Saturday, 3rd October 1998 and has become part of the house. Left, Rosalind Myers serves one of her last customers Mrs. Margaret Suddaby before the shop's closure a few days later.

Although many villagers remember the annual Royal British Legion children's outing, it may come as quite a surprise to learn that it was in name only. In order to gain charity status it was necessary to go under the Legion's name, but the trips which started c.1950, were entirely organised and funded by the efforts of the Gratton family. Patrica Gratton recalls the countless jumble sales they held in order to help raise some of the money needed. Usually, the destinations chosen were Bridlington or Scarborough. Fred Gratton cheerfully recalls that, " Every child in the village, from a baby in arms up to school leaving age had the opportunity to go on the annual excursion. Adults were charged 5 shillings each to help cover costs. However, when we arrived at the seaside, every child on the trip was given half a crown for ice-cream." Tickets for the trips were sold by the Gratton family and through Mary Thornham's shop in Church Street. Silver Wing coaches from North Cave provided the transport. Seen above are the assembled village children and their families eagerly awaiting the start of an annual trip to the seaside. The last trip which the Gratton family organised was in 1968 and required a total of 13 coaches.

Opposite the Town Hall during the Edwardian era was Mrs. Ward's bakery shop at No. 75, Market Place. Her husband Harry was the village plumber and glazier and had worked on the MacTurk's water system for South Cave. In 1914 they moved to the Bear Inn and were the licensees for many years. The shop then became the South Cave village post office, seen here at the bottom left of this photograph. It is now an antique shop known as "The Copper Shop". Anne Featherstone, the proprietor decided on the name after an old lock-up gaol was discovered on the premises following the removal of some old

shop fittings. The cell with its thick walls, small window and heavy door still exists. In times past if anyone caused trouble, they were put in this cell overnight and then transported the next morning in a horse and cart to the police station at Brough to answer to a local magistrate. The request for a lock-up house at South Cave was made on the 17th October 1843 to the Clerk of the Peace of the East Riding of Yorkshire under the act for the appointment and payment of Parish Constables. A little further up is Bank House at No. 91, Market Place now occupied by Mr. and Mrs. R. D. Lucas, who have mortgage deeds dated 1767 referring to their property as a former brewhouse known as the Blue Bell Inn. By 1830 the premises had become the offices of a solicitor Mr. Joseph Blanchard Burland. In 1893 the practice was known as Burland and MacTurk, Solicitors. Mr. Peter Frederick Bilton was the last solicitor at Bank House and he closed his offices there in 1992.

Public Houses

In 1750 there were some eight or nine public houses in South Cave, although by 1825 this number had fallen to six. The King's Head, Half Moon, Blue Bell, Rose and Crown, the Blacksmith's Arms, (later The Prince Albert,) the Bay Horse (at West End), the Windmill and the Three Tuns were among some of the former inns that have long since disappeared from the village.

The Fox and Coney and the Bear Inn are now the only two remaining hostelries and both are in the Market Place almost opposite each other. The Bear Inn is so named in recognition of the Barnard family whose coat of arms includes "the bear". Besides their social function, these inns were places where business was transacted and where the village Friendly Societies and various committees congregated for discussions.

At the rear of the Bear Inn was once a large wooden hut which was used for a variety of activities including the dressing room for the village football team, the headquarters of the Home Guard and as a place in which the South Cave Subscription Silver Band could practice. The hut had originally been built as a Catholic Chapel for the Irish "navvies" who worked on the construction of the Hull and Barnsley West Junction Railway in the 1880s.

Top, the old hut at the rear of the Bear Inn which was demolished in 1964. Dating back to the time the hut was used as a chapel there is a grave stone nearby which marks the last resting place of Robert William the son of Robert and Hannah Russell who died in 1865 aged 6 months. The child's father is thought to have been a railway employee.

South Cave Football Team, winners of Division II East Riding Amateur League and East Riding Intermediate Cup, taken outside the Bear Inn during the 1927-28 season. For many years the football pitch was in a grass field adjoining Cow Pasture and Cliffs Lane on Beverley Road. In March 1900 a tragedy occurred whilst South Cave and Hull Victoria football teams were playing a match on the village pitch. William J. Walford, a wood carver from St. Luke Street, Hull who was playing for the South Cave team inexplicably died during the game. It was reported that the South Cave Football Team raised a subscription for his family.

Top, a party of cyclists stopping at the Fox and Coney c.1905. Above, a much later view of the Fox and Coney. This inn dates from 1739 when it was owned by a Mr. Hardy and served as a coaching house. It is recorded as The Fox in 1764 but became known as the Fox and Coney during the late 18th century when William Goodlad was the innkeeper. He was also a furrier and farmer as well as the village postmaster. For many years the inn belonged continuously to various breweries but in 1993 it passed once again into private ownership.

Right, a bill for drinks from Monday, 2nd April 1810. The Fox and Coney was also an Excise and Post Office as well as a coaching station at this time. The landlord was a Barnard Cook, (1760-1840), who in May 1829 was arrested for unpaid debts and sent to prison. He later became landlord of the Blacksmith's Arms in the Market Place in 1831 until 1833.

COOK's FOX AND CONEY, And EXCISE-OFFICE, SOUTH-CAVE.	£.	s.	d.
Dinner			
Wine		10	—
Negus and Punch	1	10	
Rum, Brandy, and Geneva			5
Coffee, Tea, &c.			
Supper			
Porter, Ale, Beer, &c.			
Tobacco			
Cyder			
Fruit			
Writing Paper			
Fire			
Servants' Eating, and Ale			
Hay and Corn			
Post-Chaise			
	£. 2	-5	-0
Rum & Brandy		2	-6
	2	-7	-0

Robert Peck, Printer, Scale-Lane, Hull.

24

The Windmill situated next door to the Town Hall was last recorded in use as a public house in 1846. This photograph was taken in 1935 during the Silver Jubilee Celebrations, when the old inn was reopened and made a central part of the events. Local man Mr. Alan Hall, an excellent horseman, re-enacted the notorious highwayman Dick Turpin's flight in 1738 from the authorities, by escaping out of a window at the Green Dragon Inn, Welton. Alan mimicked the escape and rode on through the village of Brough jumping over the toll bar gate which had been especially re-erected for the occasion. He then went on to South Cave where he stopped at the Windmill, which Turpin was reputed to have frequented on his visits to the area, on the notion that his horse needed to be reshod by the resident blacksmith, here played by Harry Youngsen. Alan Hall as Dick Turpin is seen enjoying a flagon of ale with the landlord played by James Freeman, Snr. While his horse was being attended to by the blacksmith, word was sent that the authorities were still hot on his trail, so the re-enactment was completed when Turpin fled through the back of the inn, quickly mounted his horse 'Black Bess' and rode away at great speed up Station Road towards Market Weighton.

Carriers outside Mr. A.W. Suddaby's grocery and drapery store in 1911. This photograph was quite likely taken by Mr. Suddaby, who in his spare time was a keen photographer. The Three Tuns was demolished c.1926 for road widening. A Co-operative Wholesale Society store was later built on part of the site.

Above an early 20th century view of the Market Place, looking south towards Brough Road.

Among the first houses to be erected beyond the older built-up area was the Lodge or Dower House (later known as Sunnyside), on the western side of Station Road. The house, made of local limestone is believed to have been constructed shortly after 1811. It was rebuilt in 1869-70 for Mrs. Elizabeth M. Barnard.

Moving up from the Market Place on the eastern side of Station Road is the former South Cave Vicarage. It was built in the Gothic style in 1845 and enlarged in 1872. In 1962 it had become too costly to maintain and was sold at auction. A new smaller vicarage was built in the grounds.

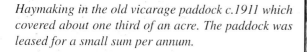

Haymaking in the old vicarage paddock c.1911 which covered about one third of an acre. The paddock was leased for a small sum per annum.

Further along the western side of Station Road are a set of entrance gates into the grounds of Cave Castle. On each side, mounted on a brick column and pedestal, is a bear sculpted in stone, seated on its haunches, symbolically keeping guard over the Barnard family domain. The bear was the main feature of the Barnard family crest as seen above left, in the coat of arms belonging to Henry Gee Barnard as heir to the estate in 1817.

Chapel and Churchyard

In 1872 when All Saints' churchyard at West End had become full, Mr. Barnard of Cave Castle, donated a little over an acre of land on the outskirts of the village on Station Road for use as a new burial ground.

The new cemetery together with the small brick chapel built in the Gothic style were consecrated in 1873 and the first internment took place on the 15th November that year which was that of a baby, William Thompson, aged 7 months.

By 1880 the old churchyard at All Saints' Church had been formally closed for any further burials. The new chapel and churchyard were transferred to the administration of the South Cave Parish Council in 1910. This churchyard was further extended in 1967. Over time the Victorian chapel fell into disuse and into a serious state of disrepair, becoming a target for vandals.

During the early 1990s there was much local debate concerning the chapel's future when the Parish Council made a controversial suggestion. This was to engage a responsible Heritage Trust which it was hoped, would restore and convert the building for use as a unique holiday home.

However, villagers strongly rejected the proposal and the Parish Council raised the necessary money needed for restoration through various sales, grants and the holding of occasional candlelight classical music concerts within the chapel itself.

Although its future use is still very much uncertain due to various legal and religious technicalities, the Parish Council's intention is to eventually bring the chapel into regular use by the whole community for a range of activities.

Above right, the South Cave Cemetery Chapel. A Victorian brass bell which tolled for the deceased and which was hung in the chapel bell turret was stolen some years ago - but was then mysteriously returned. It was discovered in 1992 in the back of a cupboard in the Town Hall having been painted black. Parish Councillor Jean Bullman and her husband Terence had the bell restored. Following the removal of paint and grime the bell was taken to the Town Hall for safe keeping along with another discovery, that of the town crier's old bell. This had also been forgotten and was subsequently discovered in a villager's home. Right, the late Councillor R. Wilson with the chapel bell.

Beverley Road

Returning to the Market Place, South Cave we see this unusual view of what is now known as Holderness House, No. 36, Market Place, situated at the junction with Beverley Road and Market Place. This photograph was taken c.1885 when the property incorporated a corner shop. The two storey grey brick building had been built in the early 19th century and was originally owned by John Holborn, Plumber and Glazier (d.1838). By 1861 it belonged to William Cousens and his eldest son Thomas who were Painters, Paperhangers, Plumbers and Gasfitters. Shortly after this photograph was taken the shop closed and the corner of the building was remodelled to include a large bay window. It became the residence of Mr. William Richardson, a solicitor's clerk, registrar and local historian. It is believed that a large portion of the Roman road to South Newbald lies adjacent to this house. In 1913 whilst excavating the Market Place for gas pipes, workmen found a pavement extending across the entire road at a depth of two feet. A similar pavement was also revealed when more gas pipes were laid some ten yards away. Further evidence of Romano-British occupation was later discovered during a house construction in 1965 at No. 85, Beverley Road when an iron-smelting site was found. Four years later, during building work quantities of pottery, coins and building stone were discovered at nearby Nos. 81 and 83, Beverley Road. Earlier in 1961 excavations in the garden of No, 81, had revealed pottery of many types (including amphora) and an inhumation covered with Roman roofing tiles.

The same view taken in 1931. This corner of Beverley Road and Market Place was known in the 18th century as Poulter or Poulterer's Hole after the poulterers who once stood there on market days selling poultry, butter and eggs from their stalls. Cattle, sheep and pigs were on sale further up and down the Market Place.

A view of Beverley Road taken from the Town Hall clock tower. The first large detached house on the left belonged to Mr. Tom Farthing who up until the 1920s made ploughs and other agricultural implements on nearby premises. The house was built in 1913 by his cousin's firm, Leeson's of Driffield and is shown below still under construction. Mr. Farthing lived in the house until his death in 1941 at the age of 81 years.

Further along Beverley Road is Little Wold Lane. This view of the corner of the lane was taken in c.1910 and shows young Dorothy Moverley in the foreground. Note the cow grazing close by. Village cow keepers were able to rent a lane or road on an annual basis and would often pay local boys a few coppers to look after some of the cows with which they had been entrusted. This practice was known as 'tenting'. In days gone by Little Wold Lane was better known as Dicky Straker Lane, for it is said that this gentleman was drowned, either by accident or suicide, in a pond situated in the lane. There was also a brickmaking works here sometime during the 18th century but it was recorded as disused by 1890. In the

garden of No. 8, Little Wold Lane (Shepherd's Well Farm), is situated the old Shepherd's Well. Before the introduction of piped water supplies the surrounding community obtained their water from this source. Many years ago the well was blocked up and a wash house built over it. In 1994 there was a public outcry following the approval of sale of nearby Little Wold Wood to create a new quarrying site. Villagers and businesses raised £18,500 in less than a month to buy the 20 acre wood instead and presented it to the Woodland Trust, a national charity, in order to preserve this important conservation area.

Mount Airy Farm

Mount Airy Farm is approached from the Beverley Road and is situated at the top of a steep hill which rises to a height of about 500 feet. It was one of the first farmsteads to be built away from the village following the Enclosure Act in the late 18th century. From the farm there are magnificent views of the River Humber and Lincolnshire to the south and across to the Vale of York.

The property had originally belonged to the Cave Castle Estate and was rented out to one farmer until the early 1920s when the farm became vacant. Due to a world recession causing poor prices for agricultural produce throughout the country it was generally difficult to find tenants to keep large farms.

Therefore, in an effort to attract new tenants the Cave Castle Estate Trustees had the farmhouse converted into two houses and the holding was also split into two parts. These became known as Mount Airy Farm North and Mount Airy Farm South.

Mr. J.W. Clark farmed the northern holding and in 1926, Mr. Sidney C. May and his wife Dolly who were originally from Crabley Creek Farm became the tenants of the southern holding. The farm holdings were later sold following the sale of the Cave Castle Estate in 1939 to a Mr. Dent. Following two more owners Mr. May finally took on both holdings making the farm into one single unit again. Lenny May was born at the farm in 1929 and remembers as a young boy during the 1930s that sharing the farm only caused a few minor problems with livestock and access.

Overall, the two families got along very well together and they would often help each other, especially around threshing time, a process which required a number of hands; engine driver, feeder, sack-man and several other men to handle the sheaves, straw, chaff and grain. Although one or two hired hands lived on the farm a few local men would be employed to help with the work and it was not unusual for the threshing crew to work a twelve hour day.

In the winter months Stan Watson of Brantingham used to hire out his threshing machine set to farmers in the area for about £1 per day plus coal and water as fuel for the engine. When required he would drive the set from Brantingham up to the farm stackyard at Mount Airy.

At 16 years old Lenny was the chaff carrier, a job which was without doubt the most unpleasant task of all on threshing day. He recalls the job entailed working in a confined space between the machine and the stack collecting the chaff or seed coverings and other debris onto a large sheet with a wooden rake. To add to this discomfort, loose corn often fell onto him from the machine, resulting in a sore neck. After twisting the corners of a full sheet together he would sling it over his shoulder and take it away to a barn where it would be stored and later used as animal fodder.

When he was a little older and in order to earn a few extra shillings, he took on a heavier job at the other end of the machine carrying bags of up to 18 stone across his shoulders a short distance and then up at least twelve steps into the granary. Only a few farm workers were capable of "carrying corn" due to the sheer weight and the fact that one hand was required to hold the mouth of the sack, thus requiring a great deal of strength and skill.

In those days at least nine people would have been required to help with harvesting and even more to help at threshing time. However, improvements in farm machinery following the Second World War such as mass produced tractors and combine harvesters radically reduced the number of farm labourers needed.

During the harsh winter of 1947 for a period of 13 weeks, the roads leading to the farm were inaccessible due to the constant snow drifts. Frequently, local men came to help dig the snow out from the road to the farm, but usually by the next day more snow had fallen. Animals were fed on complete oats since it had been impossible to get the threshing machine up from Brantingham to thresh the straw.

The May family constructed a wooden sledge to enable them to get into South Cave. Sidney's wife Dolly used the sledge, which was pulled by a horse across the fields to bring provisions from the village such as flour which came in 8 stone sacks.

Lenny recalls that his mother was quite enterprising when in the 1930s she started to rear her own turkeys on the farm. At Christmas they were all plucked and delivered round the district and some years her sales exceeded those of the farm. In fact Dolly was so successful that Mr. Twydale of Twydale Turkeys, Driffield sought her help to manage his turkey farm since he needed her expertise. However, as she had six children to care for she had to decline his offer of employment.

When Sidney retired in 1974 Mount Airy Farm was passed to his son Lenny who now farms it with his son Neil.

Situated below Mount Airy farmland in a plantation known locally as "The Cliffs" we see members of a shooting party gathered around an old railway carriage which was used for many years as a shooting lodge and was inhabited by the estate gamekeeper. Shooters and beaters would stop for their lunch here during a days shoot but beaters were segregated into one end of the carriage whilst the guns had the other half. It is not known from where the disused railway carriage was acquired though it was towed by traction engine to this spot in March 1907 by Tom and Harry Watson of Brantingham. A terrible tragedy happened when the carriage, weighing over 2 tons and resting on temporary wooden chocks following the removal of its wheels, collapsed and fatally crushed Robert Goodwill, a 54 year old builder from South Cave who had crawled underneath it to commence building the permanent brick supports. Although still visible, the former lodge now lies unused and neglected.

Two milestones weathered and worn but still visible along the Beverley Road. The writing on the left-hand stone reads, "Hull to South Cave 10 miles". The right-hand stone recently suffered damage when a motor vehicle accidently bumped into it, resulting in a large fracture breaking it into two pieces. The top half was later found in the beck, but fortunately it was able to be restored. Although now extremely worn, it once gave the distance to Beverley as 7 miles.

Church Street

Above, Kiln Row Cottages situated in Market Lane, now known as Church Street, near to the junction with Market Place. These properties had been built of local stone in c.1790 on the site of a former malt kiln. However, by the late 19th century they had become notoriously overcrowded and were demolished in 1897. Shown below right, are Victoria Cottages which were subsequently constructed on the same site by the Barnard family. The chapel-like building a little further past the cottages is the old Temperance Society building. On the left in this photograph taken in 1922 is an old 17th century single storey butcher's shop which was formerly attached to the old Three Tuns public house, both buildings now demolished.

Many householders owned and killed at least one pig each year. It was not an uncommon sight to see a pig being driven down the street to the local butchers to be slaughtered. The family in this 1903 photograph would have been taking their pig only a little further round the corner into Church Street to Arthur Smith's butchers shop . The pig's carcase would be cut into hams, shoulders, flitches and chines. Once home, the meat would then be rubbed thoroughly with salt and placed in a tub, then the hams and sides of bacon were hung to dry in the warm kitchen, following which they were covered in white drawstring muslin bags to keep them clean. It was a well known saying that "nothing was ever wasted but the squeal." Liver, kidney and small cuts of pork, known collectively as "Fries" would be sent on dishes to certain friends and relatives, whilst the trimmings would be cut up and minced for pork pies and sausages. It was the tradition for dishes to be returned unwashed or bad luck would ensue. All oddments such as feet, ears, tail and bones were put into a huge earthernware jar and cooked in the oven until evening, when the bones were removed and the conglomeration was seasoned and put into basins to set as "souse" otherwise known as brawn. During the whole day a pig was killed a cauldron containing simmering fat would hang over the fire. This would eventually be the family's supply of lard for a year, which would be stored in a zinc bucket and covered with greaseproof paper.

Established 1886.

A. SMITH,
BUTCHER.
Church Street, South Cave.

PURVEYOR OF ENGLISH MEAT
—ONLY—

Pickled Beef and Tongues always on hand.

ALL HOME KILLED AND
ONLY ONE QUALITY—
THE BEST.

PORK SAUSAGE   ::   ::   A SPECIALITY.

Phone : 20Y3 North Cave.

VAN DELIVERY.

Many older villagers remember Arthur Smith's butchers shop at No. 23, Church Street. Slaughtering was done at the back of the premises, usually on a Monday. Ray Warcup recalls that when he was a young boy during the early 1930s, he and other boys would often see the blood running down into the beck and then eagerly wait for one of the slaughtermen to bring them out a pig's bladder. There would then ensue a fight as to who would get the bladder and the lucky boy who managed to get possession would then blow it up so that they could use it to play football. Practical and financial difficulties in keeping pace with hygiene regulations have meant that the majority of the small butchers who used to kill livestock and hang their own meat now buy it directly from meat wholesalers.

Below right, an advertisement for Sydney Scott's chemist shop at No. 27, Church Street dated 1930. In 1933 the business was taken over by Walter Brumfield (1907-88), whose premises can be seen in this prewar photograph. A qualified chemist, he also sold household goods and bicycles. During the Second World War Mr. Brumfield was an air raid warden. One of the first local casualties of the war was a woman walking by Cave Castle's perimeter wall when an enemy aircraft's stray bullet ricocheted off it into her cheek. "Mr. and Mrs. B." as they were locally known treated her as they would

anyone who asked for advice or medical assistance if a doctor was not available. Their reputation for providing this help became well known and as a consequence "Mr. B." was asked to give a talk on the 'Life of a Country Chemist' on the wireless on the B.B.C. Home Service in Leeds. The family moved to larger premises, after the war, on the corner of Market Place, South Cave, which became known locally as "Brummy's Corner" where village folk would stand to discuss daily affairs. "Mr. B's" former premises at No. 27, Church Street were used as the village post office until it moved in the early 1950s to its present site at Goodwill House in the Market Place. "Mr. B." made all his own handcream, cough mixture and bath salts amongst other remedies and would deliver orders on certain days to the surrounding farms and villages and to customers who were unable to visit his shop. He was also a parish councillor and later became Chairman of the Parish Council for

many years. "Mr. B" and his wife Nancy were also founder members of the local bowling club. "Mr. B" was chairman of the committee which founded and built the Sports Hall in 1978 in Church Street, South Cave. Mr. and Mrs. Brumfield's chemist shop was sold on their retirement in the early 1970s to Selles Dispensing Chemists who still run it today.

Above, an advertisement for Mary Thornham's shop, which was situated at No.31, Church Street. It had formerly been Fred Moore's saddlery and cobblers shop. Mary bought the shop from Mrs. Moore in 1965. The shop sold haberdashery, drapery and ironmongery goods as well as knitting wools, shoes, and wellingtons. In 1982 Mary sold the shop to a Mr. Wilson of North Cave who kept the shop open for a further three years after which it became a private residence.

The Temperance Society

A Temperance Society existed in South Cave from at least 1854. As part of the national temperance movement, it was dedicated to curtailing the consumption of alcohol by total prohibition, local restriction, or encouragement of declarations of personal abstinence or promises of good intention more commonly known as *"The Pledge."*

The Society was closely allied to the Independent and Wesleyan Chapels and the secretary and committee were usually active nonconformists. Initially, local enrolment was quite high with some 174 members recorded in 1855. However, subscriptions proved difficult to collect and by 1861 membership had fallen drastically with only 21 regular members attending the society meetings.

In 1856, land was bought in Church Street and a Temperance Hall erected at a cost of £145. 10s. 5d. This modest brick building was regularly used by enthusiastic visiting circuit speakers, encouraging those who came to listen to totally abstain from the evils of drink. One of the well known "ditties" of the day was,

> *"Dare to be a Daniel,*
> *Dare to be alone,*
> *Dare to pass a public house,*
> *And leave the beer alone."*

By 1859 a Temperance Hotel had opened at number 50, Market Place. The proprietor was Timothy Dunn, who was also a farmer and horse dealer. By 1861 it was no longer in existence, perhaps the majority of travellers preferring to stay at the Fox and Coney which was situated next door. Another Temperance Hotel was opened by John Waudby in Church Street in c.1883, but like the earlier hotel his business did not survive for very long.

The annual Good Friday Temperance Tea held on land near to what is now known as Nunnery Walk in the West End of the village was always extremely well attended. In 1868, one hundred and eighty three tickets at a cost of 1/- each were sold and four stones of ham, six stones of plum bread, seven stones of plain bread, just over 18 pounds of butter and three pounds of tea were consumed.

Members of the Waudby family were prominent activists of the Society and would often try and drum up interest on the steps of the Town Hall. Not everyone took kindly to these lectures, one such opponent being George Martin, (son of Obed, who had a butcher's shop in the Market Place during the 19th century), known locally as *"Hook Martin"*.

Even at the age of seventy George would throw his hat up in the air in disgust at the sight of these earnest attempts to turn locals against alcohol and would try his best to incite Mr. John Waudby or anyone else to fight him. Despite the pleas of those nearest him not to make a fuss, he would shout, *" I'll fight the best man here. I'd be more inclined to have a drink of gin than listen to a temperance lecture."*

Apparently, even many younger local men were afraid of him and his challenges to a fight were never taken up. The police would often rely on George to move unwanted travellers, which he was more than pleased to do.

The Electric Cinema

The Temperance Society had disbanded by 1918 but later a local Boys' Club used the former meeting hall. In c.1930 it was bought by Bob Alcock and Allan Moore who converted it into a cinema house. The owners had previously used the Church Institute to show silent films, but when talking pictures were introduced they were keen to move to more suitable premises. The refurbished building included a sound system, modern seats and an inclined floor.

Geoff Grice, Bob Alcock's nephew recalls in 1933 when he was 12 years old, he was invited to sit through a practice run of a film, before it was shown to the public. He duly arrived and took his seat in the empty hall. The lights went down and Geoff settled down to watch," The *Mystery of the Wax Museum."* Rated as a notable horror film for its day, both for the use of Technicolor and art direction it also had the novelty of sound.

The plot for a young boy was, however, too much to bear. The beginning of the film involved a fire with lifelike figures melting into a grisly ooze, followed by scenes set in a city morgue at night, with a dead body suddenly popping up as a side-effect of embalming fluid; not to mention the ghoulish sculptor chasing through shadows collecting bodies for his exhibition. Geoff was so frightened, he leapt from his seat and ran out at great speed straight into a closed door. He recalls, *" I was absolutely terrified and I couldn't get out of the hall quick enough."*

In late 1947 following the untimely death of Allan at the age of 42 years, Bob Alcock sold the cinema to a Mr. Prendergast from York who also owned a number of other cinemas. Roy and Freda Ward managed it with a staff of two, Ellen Crowther who was the usherette and John Thornham who was the projectionist. Later Mr. Prendergast changed its use to that of a Bingo Hall. The building was later sold and converted into the branch premises of the Larards Estate Agency.

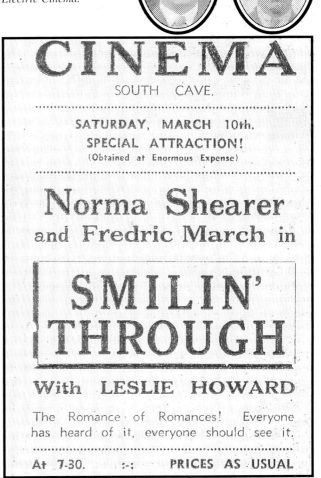

From the left, Bob Alcock and Allan Moore, the original proprietors of the Electric Cinema.

CINEMA
SOUTH CAVE.

SATURDAY, MARCH 10th.
SPECIAL ATTRACTION!
(Obtained at Enormous Expense)

Norma Shearer
and Fredric March in

SMILIN' THROUGH

With LESLIE HOWARD

The Romance of Romances! Everyone has heard of it, everyone should see it.

At 7-30.   :-:   PRICES AS USUAL

Above, a 1932 poster from the early days of Alcock and Moore's Picture House.

Archie Ernest Trout

Archie Ernest Trout lived in South Cave for many years until his death in 1962. During his lifetime he became well known as both a writer and speaker on many general subjects and was regarded as an authoritative historian on his adopted home of South Cave and the surrounding villages. He regularly gave public lectures and tours on local historical topics of interest.

Archie was born on the 2nd September 1879 at number 16, Wilberforce Terrace, Argyll Street, Hull, into a family that was staunchly Methodist, temperate and self-improving. These were to be his characteristics also and to influence him throughout his life.

At the age of 12 years he began work in the office of Michael Kelly, the Secretary and Superintendent of the Hull General Cemetery. Eighteen months later, Archie left, joining the London North Western Railway as a junior in the Goods Department, from where he was steadily promoted to a Collector of Accounts in 1909 and then Chief of Accounts in 1924.

On Wednesday, 18th September 1901 Archie married Florence Dixon whom he had met at the Fountain Road Methodist Mission in Hull, where they were both members. Their only son Ernest was born the following year.

The family moved to the village of South Cave in August 1910. Their intention had initially been to help nurse Florence's sister back to good health and then return to Hull, but they liked the village so much they stayed. Other than an interval of just over five years, they lived in the village for the rest of their lives.

Archie soon found much of historical interest in South Cave and the neighbouring villages. Consequently he quickly acquired a considerable knowledge of the area often taking visiting societies on historical tours of the locality. It was once said of Archie that he was,

"A gifted and willing speaker with a sense of humour, he was in frequent demand by local groups and societies."

He became an active member of the local Congregational Chapel at West End and occasionally attended the Wesleyan Chapel in Church Street. This was the street in which he lived with his family in a double-fronted Victorian house known as "South View," now number 16.

During the First World War Archie was not accepted for war service owing to his poor health although he remained employed by the railway company. Interestingly, between 1916-1923 he maintained a diary which ran into some four volumes. Among the pages of the diary we get glimpses of Archie's hopes, disappointments and triumphs concerning his family, his work, and social activities.

Throughout the diary it is clearly evident that Archie took a great interest in the affairs of South Cave and was instrumental in raising local concern and funds to pay for a village street gas lamp known as the "Hobbies" street gas lamp.

Whist Drives and dances were held in aid of funds for the lamp which was installed in 1921 outside number 32, Market Place. Each evening the "lamplighter man" (Tom Gibson in later years), would walk up Church Street to the Market Place with his special long pole. This had a hook on the end to pull a lever which lit the lamp and in the morning the process was reversed. The gas lamp was in use until 1952 when electric

Archie Ernest Trout

lighting was adopted and some 28 electric lights were installed around the village.

Another of Archie's hobbies was collecting stamps and coins. He later developed this interest into research and writing on the topic of postal history. As well as an in-depth study of the Bradford district postal history, he wrote articles on the postal services of South Cave, Everthorpe and North Cave.

In fact included in Archie's prolific output of articles and manuscripts on various subjects and places, many were concerning South Cave and district. These were either sold or given to the Hull Central Library (Local History) in 1934, prior to his departure on promotion to Bradford as Chief Accounts Clerk for that district. Some of his writings on the South Cave area include such titles as,

"An Old Yorkshire Congregation, South Cave Congregational Church"; "Cheesecake Day at Cave"; "An old East Yorkshire Market Place"; "South Cave Postal History"; "Fields Gardens and Lanes of South Cave"; "South Cave and the Washingtons"; "Men and Books of South Cave"; "Rules and Orders of the Friendly Society of South Cave, 1802" and "Notes on South Cave Castle."

Following his retirement in 1939, Archie and Florence moved back to their home "South View," Church Street, South Cave which they had rented out whilst living in Bradford.

After many years of peaceful retirement in South Cave, Florence, following a short period of ill-health, passed away on the 2nd March 1959 and was buried at the South Cave cemetery. A Mrs. Rignall who was taken on by Archie as a housekeeper looked after him until his death three years later on the 20th June 1962.

Archie's great grandson, Edwin Trout, inherited many of his papers and in 1994 took on the difficult task of creating a comprehensive bibliography of his great grandfather's published works, which number some seventy-seven articles. He also wrote an informative account of Archie's life from which some of the material contained in this account has been drawn.

Right, Margaret, daughter of Ben and Mary Ann Waudby is seen here standing at the gate of Wesley Farm with her two young brothers Ted, left and Thomas (Tot),who at the age of 23 died in Leeds General Infirmary from serious wounds sustained in combat during the First World War. Wesley Farm was sold in 1964, following the retirement of Ted. By 1966 it had been demolished to make way for a new housing development. Below, Margaret Waudby feeding the chickens.

Wesley Close and Castle Rise now stand on the site of the former farm. The Waudby family were well known in the village and seen here back row from left to right are, William, Samuel, Harold, Frederick, Benjamin (farmer at Wesley Close and father of Margaret, Thomas and Ted), Walter (Sub-Postmaster), Front row, Thomas (tailor), Molly, June and John Waudby (Primitive Methodist preacher and tailor).

Left, nearby was Parkside Farm. This photograph was taken from Bacchus Lane looking onto the rear of the Girls' School in Church Street, c.1952. Although the farmhouse still exists as a private dwelling the land was sold about 1980 for the building of a sheltered housing development which is known as "Wold View".

Left, South Cave Cricket Club 1907. The club is believed to have been formed during the mid-19th century. The East Yorkshire Book of Cricket records the club as having played a match against Cherry Burton in 1864. For many years the club played in a field to the rear of Wesley Farm, Church Street, before moving to a new site complete with a large white painted pavilion on the south west side of Little Wold Lane. In November 1949 the Ministry of Education confirmed the award of a grant to the newly formed South Cave Social and Recreational Committee of £540 which went towards the purchase of Bull Field, part of the Cave Castle Estate. Following the levelling of the field in the spring of 1950 the Cricket Club moved to this site along with the South Cave Football Club who both still share the site. The Tennis and Bowls Clubs were formed in 1950 and are located on nearby land which is also held in trust by the South Cave Social and Recreational Committee.

Above, by the turn of the 19th century South Cave had its own Boys' Brigade and for a number of years an annual camp was held in the cricket field at the rear of Wesley Farm. Several companies from the Hull Boys' Brigade would also be in attendance. Displays of drill and gymnastics were given to the public during their stay. This particular display shown right was given in 1907.

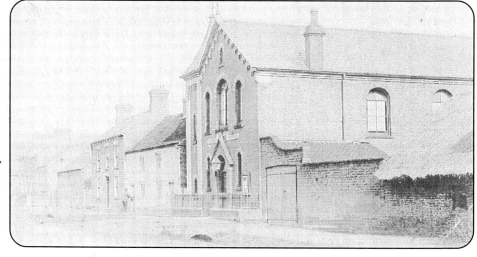

Right, the old Primitive Chapel. John Waudby (1851-1938), the village tailor was a Primitive Methodist preacher for over fifty years and became the second preacher to the minister on the North Cave Circuit. In 1929 he was still actively preaching and working at the age of 78 years. The secret of his good health he said was the fact, " Of never having had a bit o' bacca, never having had a drop o' drink, and of liking employment."

Methodism

The officially recognised religion of England in the 18th century was Anglicanism and those who chose to worship in any other way were known as Nonconformists. These "Dissenters", as they were also known, were barely tolerated and it was not until 1750 that they were allowed any measure of real freedom to worship as they desired.

One of the most well known proponents of nonconformism was the great evangelist John Wesley, (1703-1791), founder of the Methodist movement. Although he was an ordained Anglican priest he never had a parish of his own but instead preferred to travel extensively around the country preaching to the public in open-air services. He is known to have preached in North Cave in July 1761 and later in June 1788 when he paid a visit to his friend the Reverend James Stillingfleet at Hotham.

By 1782, Methodism had become well established in South Cave. The home of George Turner was licensed as their meeting house and in 1790 Richard Milner's house in Church Street was similarly registered. In June 1816 a Wesleyan Chapel in Church Street was opened for Divine Worship.

However, despite the refurbishment of the interior and a new Sunday School room being added during the 1880s, it is evident that the chapel had difficulty in supporting itself financially. During its centenary year of 1916 a notice was issued by the Ministers to local people to raise funds to help to repay a debt of £25 which was still outstanding from the cost of the renovations some twenty years earlier.

The chapel continued to be used for public worship until its closure in 1943 as a result of falling membership. For a number of years afterwards the building was occupied by the Healey brothers for their light engineering business before later becoming a garage.

Following John Wesley's death in 1791, Methodism began to split into factions. The Primitive faction was formed in 1810 by William Clowes and Hugh Bourne. Clowes was known in his time as a gifted evangelical speaker and began preaching tours in the area in 1819. He preached in South Cave twice during that particular year. Taken from his journal is the following extract,

"On Sunday February 28th I rode eight miles, walked ten, preached three times and heard two sermons. The places officiated were at Elloughton in the morning, South Cave in the afternoon and North Cave in the evening. In the afternoon, at South Cave, in the open air, the congregation was very great and the power of Jehovah rested on the living mass of human beings, all was still as evening and many wept."

The old Primitive Methodist Church can be seen on the left in this view of Church Street.

1816=1916.

The Centenary of Methodism in South Cave

will be celebrated in the
WESLEYAN CHAPEL, SOUTH CAVE,
on THURSDAY, AUGUST 3rd, 1916.

Divine Worship at 4-15.   Preacher—

Rev. SAMUEL CHADWICK
(of Cliff College, Sheffield).

PUBLIC TEA at 5-30
in the Primitive Methodist Schoolroom (kindly lent for the occasion.)   Tickets 1/- each.

Public Meeting at 7 o'clock.   Chairman—
SIR ALFRED GELDER, M.P.

Speakers—
REV. SAMUEL CHADWICK,
supported by Rev. C. H. Daniel, M.A., Rev. R. Brotherton, and the Circuit Ministers.

Collections in aid of Centenary Effort.

A Primitive Methodist Society was begun soon after Clowes visit, although it was not until 1837 that a Primitive Methodist or "Ranters" Chapel was built in the village. It was situated behind two cottages in Church Street.

The old chapel and cottages were demolished in 1876 and on the same site a new chapel with a schoolroom was erected the following year at a cost of about £600. The chapel later united with the local Wesleyan society and still serves as a thriving Methodist Chapel in the village.

The Primitives or "Ranters" had been disowned by the main body of Wesleyans partly because of their irregular meetings and enthusiastic forms of worship. Pictured right, Mr. William Nicholson of Beverley was one such excitable Primitive worshipper. Better known as "Praying Billy" he would go into public houses around the district and loudly proclaim to all assembled there that beer was the "Devil's Broth." It is known that while he was praying in front of a butcher's shop near the Three Tuns public house on the corner of Church Street, South Cave, the butcher threw a bucket of water over him.

The Women's Institute was introduced into Great Britain from Canada in 1915 and by 1939 there were about six thousand W.I.s throughout the country. The movement provided invaluable support during the Second World War, particularly in respect of the production of foodstuffs. The South Cave branch of the W.I. was formed in 1929 and members held their meetings in the old Temperance Hall in Church Street until they obtained their own premises. Above and below, ladies of the South Cave Women's Institute at the opening of their wooden hut in 1930. The hut had belonged to the army and was brought from Rolston, near Hornsea. The purchase of it together with transport and re-erection costs totalled £120.

Right, a bazaar and garden fete notice dated June 1930. The event was held at Drewton Manor to raise the funds needed to pay for the hut and its furnishings. Below, in 1982 work began building a brick exterior wall to the wooden hut which was completed by the summer of 1983.

PROGRAMME.

BAZAAR

.: AND :.

GARDEN FÊTE

AT

Drewton Manor,
SOUTH CAVE.

ON

SATURDAY, 28th JUNE,
1930.

OBJECT OF FÊTE.

To raise Funds to meet the cost of
"The Hut" and furnishing.

Proceedings to be opened at 2-30 p.m. by

MRS. FIELD-TILL,
ELLERKER HALL.

President : BASIL E. MAXSTED, Esq., J.P.

Supported by :

Major W. H. Carver, M.P.   F. Noble Wood, Esq.
Mrs. Carver.   Mrs. Breazley, Brough.
Mrs. Percy Lambert, Brough, and others.

Grand Musical Programme by

THE SOUTH CAVE SILVER BAND.

Conductor : Mr. F. Moore.

A view of Church Street in 1901. The schoolboy on his way home is William Cousens aged 8 years. The open beck was covered over in the early 1960s. On the right, the gates of Wesley Farm are visible and to the left a little further down the street jutting out is the Church Institute, a small grey brick Gothic style building erected in September 1883 by the South Cave Branch of the Church of England Temperance Society. Much of the money raised to pay for the building was obtained by the issuing of prospectuses, which resulted in a large number of shares being taken. The Institute and a bazaar were opened by Mr. Charles E.G.B. Barnard of Cave Castle who said that he, " ... trusted the Institute would be of great service and benefit to the inhabitants of South Cave and neighbourhood." A friendly society known as the Allen Jackson Lodge of Druids used to meet at the Institute in the old reading room at the back of the hall. The Druids would hold an annual concert in the Institute in order to obtain new members and at the annual club feast they would parade around the village with the brass band in attendance. During the mid-1920s Geoff Grice remembers his uncle Bob Alcock putting up a big sheet on the washing line at the back of his father's veterinary practice at No. 50, Market Place where he gave a free film show to friends and neighbours. Encouraged by the reaction, he set up in partnership with Allan Moore and opened the very first modern cinema in the Church Institute. A small enclosed projector room was constructed and fitted to the outside front wall of the Institute. The projector itself went through a window and the audience sat on wooden seats to watch silent films which were accompanied by 'Old Sandy' Sanderson who added drama to the action via his piano. During the early 1930s the cinema moved to what was formerly a Temperance Hall in Church Street. At the present time the Institute is primarily used as a Playgroup for under 5 year old children.

Number 53, Church Street has the distinction of being the last thatched property in South Cave to be converted to a tiled roof. Here we see George Smith with his family, c.1915 standing outside the property which was then his cobblers shop. He was also at one time the village postman. Throughout the 19th and early 20th centuries there were a number of boot and shoemakers in the village. The Smith, Thompson and Thornham families were the most prominent in that particular occupation.

For many years a Youth Club thrived at the Church Institute. It was founded in 1948 by Mr. Stan Daniel, the headmaster of the Boys' School. He organised the Christmas pantomimes between 1953-57, in which the young people entertained the village folk. Ernest Skipsey usually played the piano. Although Stan departed in 1957 the Youth Club continued in existence for several more years under the charge of a Mr. Harris. Above, the 1954 production of Robinson Crusoe.

CAST OF CHARACTERS

Robinson Crusoe	Jean Gibson	Mulligatawny	M. Storey
Sam Snorer	Marcia Smith	Kedgeree	Cynthia Freeman
Bob Down	Gillian Hyde	Captain Crossbones	Ken Noble
Ma Fidler	Norman Elliott	Johnny Windup	K Cleminshaw
Eulalia	Wendy Cousens	Wall-Eye Willy	Garry Hyde
Pepits	Enid Waudby	Mutineers	B. Hurd, P. Smith
Captain Cummango	G. Harrison	Cannibals	E. Young, G. Kirk
Juanita	Marlene Alcock	Brazillian Girls ...	B. Lindley
Don Ramon Lupez			M. Foster, H. Jewitt
Hernado de Soto	John Elliott		
Man Friday	Colin Taylor		

Taken in December 1918 this photograph shows Miss Maggie Hobson schoolmistress with girls from Mrs. Barnard's school dressed in their Christmas play costumes.

42

Girls' School

Pupils from old Girls' School taken c.1933.

In 1844, Mrs. Elizabeth Mary Barnard established a girls' school on a site now occupied by numbers 12 and 14 Market Place. A public lending library was annexed to it in 1845. In 1865, Mrs. Barnard replaced what had become inadequate premises with a purpose built school together with a schoolmistress's house on land purchased from Mr. John Waudby in Church Street.

Every summer Mrs. Barnard invited all the school children from the village up to the castle gardens to pick and eat their fill of ripe gooseberries although no fruit was allowed to be taken away. At Christmas pupils personally received a brown paper bag full of seasonal fare which included a mince pie, an orange, apple and a few sweets.

Following Mrs. Barnard's death in 1872 her niece Miss Sophia Letitia Barnard supervised the running of the school. As a result of the Education Act of 1902, Miss. Barnard appointed herself and three others as foundation managers and leased the school to them for one shilling per annum and the house and playground at an annual rent of £15. 0s 0d.

Up until her death Miss Barnard gave two prizes annually to each standard in school. This took the form of money of up to 3s 6d. which was invested for the girls in the Yorkshire Penny Bank. By her will of 1910 she left the Girls' and Boys' schools to the York Diocesan Trust, thereby ending a century's close involvement by the Barnard family in the education of South Cave children.

Former pupils of the school remember their time there with great fondness. Many especially recall the Horlicks which Miss Florence J. Dennis, Headmistress made for all her pupils at playtime, before the Second World War.

In 1934 seven year old Janke Maryke Baarda came from Holland to live at South Cave. A week after arriving her mother took her to the girls' school. As Janke (known as Jannie), was unable to speak a word of English, Miss Dennis placed her in Miss Carrie Johnson's infants class where she found learning a new language very strange. Other children quickly made friends with her and would ask how various words were pronounced in Dutch and gradually her English improved. It was not long before she was able to join her own age group.

Jannie disliked being different from the other girls and felt embarrassed when local visitors to the school such as Major William Henton Carver, Mrs. Margaret Radcliffe or the School Inspectors regularly singled her out asking, *"And how is the little Dutch girl?"*

On the occasion of the Silver Jubilee of King George V and Queen Mary in May 1935 when, as part of the celebrations all the village children paraded around South Cave in fancy dress, it was much to Jannie's disappointment that her mother made her wear a Dutch costume. Three years later Jannie moved to Riccall, near Selby with her parents, leaving the school and South Cave with many happy memories.

In 1952 the senior school children in the village were transferred to Hessle, the boys' school becoming a junior school and the girls' school being used for infants. In 1967 both schools closed and a new primary school opened further along Church Street. The old girls' school was later sold by the York Diocesan Trust following which it was converted into a private house.

The old Girls' School which has now been converted into a house.

43

Right, Jannie in her Dutch costume with her parents Klaas and Geertje Baarda. She would often wear her clogs for playing in the garden of Bank House, No. 91, Market Place, part of which her father rented. One day she was asked by her mother to fetch some cream from Moate's Farm. Clip clopping down the road she soon attracted a great deal of attention and by the time she reached home there was quite a retinue of followers behind. The clogs were kicked off and she refused to wear them ever again. Jannie's parents had come from Holland to settle in South Cave at the invitation of Arthur Godfrey who was a farmer and potato merchant in the West End of the village. Mr. Godfrey wished to be introduced to the Dutch method of growing tomatoes and lettuce having been greatly impressed by Edward Baarda, (Jannie's uncle), who had arrived two years previously setting up a market garden in the nearby village of Elloughton. Edward Baarda was revolutionising market gardening methods in the area, by using his imported Dutch lights (mobile greenhouses) and introducing intensive methods of cultivation. Following a period of employment as foreman for Mr. Godfrey, Klaas rented some land on Beverley Road and started up his own business. In 1938, the family left South Cave for Riccall, near Selby where Klaas had been offered a much larger plot of land with better water supply facilities.

Below, viewing from the left in this photograph, taken just before demolition, can be seen the old joiner's shop, blacksmith shop, woodshed and a larger joiner's shop of T. W. Gibson & Company Ltd., The business was started in Church Street in about 1851 by William Gibson who was previously employed by George Petfield, a local joiner and wheelwright. It would appear that William (George's son-in-law), took over the business following George's retirement. After William died the business passed to successive family members. During the 1930s Leonard Gibson who was the joiner, wheelwright, painter and decorator as well as undertaker, employed his sons George as a blacksmith and Thomas as a joiner. Len (jnr), lived next door to the business and ran a small farm, but he would occasionally assist with joinery or undertaking work if required. Walter, another son, did not work for the family business, being employed at Capper Pass & Son Ltd., smelting works at Melton. Following Leonard's death in 1945 his son Thomas took over the company, which was then amalgamated with Arthur Gibson of Hull, a relative. However, the partnership was eventually dissolved and following Thomas's retirement in the early 1960s the business was taken over by his son Richard and nephew John Gibson along with his son Bruce. They later changed its use to a motor garage. Some years later the garage was demolished and a private residence now stands on the site.

Above, Mr. Ian Gibson, son of Walter Gibson. In 1945, as a young lad of 14 years, Ian was apprenticed to his uncle Thomas for several years to learn the joinery trade. He was one of the last members of the Gibson family to work for the joinery business before it was changed over in the 1960s to a motor services garage.

Gibson's Service Station in the 1970s, now demolished.

Mill Hill Cottage (also known as Frog Hall), is an 18th century property, originally built by the Reverend John King. It is situated on the southern side of Church Street. In 1851 M. and J. Barnby kept a boarding school here and it is believed that the ghost of a former pupil still haunts the property. Some time ago a friend of the present owners of the property witnessed the ghost of a young girl with pig tails and dressed in a white smock slide down the bannister rail and then simply disappear. In the late 19th century it was an estate house owned by the Barnards and during this period the property was much altered in a 'romantic' style. In 1947 the house was bought by Mr. Tommy Goodwill, one of the Goodwill brothers who were responsible for the building of many South Cave properties. During his occupancy a number of alterations to the house and land were made. There is mention of the existence of a windmill in the 1740s which was probably situated near to the property. The late local historian Archie Trout, wrote in 1934 that the name Frog Hall was probably derived from, "The annual migration of frogs, many scores of them, along Church Street, passing this spot, sometimes a large one with a smaller one upon its back."

Cave Castle

The present Cave Castle is a Grade II listed building constructed of stone and brick and is three storeys in height. It is approached by drives through its extensive parklands and grounds. The Castle was constructed in the early 19th century on the site of East Hall Manor House one of the two former medieval manor houses of South Cave.

The earlier East Hall Manor House was purchased in 1748 by Leuyns Boldero, a lawyer from Pontefract, West Yorkshire. In 1759 he instigated a survey of his land and property and in his own handwriting recorded, *"There is no doubt that judging from the thickness of the walls and the structure of the foundations that the building is of ancient origin."* It was his opinion that the East Hall Manor House (known to have been in existence in 1525), had in fact replaced an even earlier fortified manor house.

Some years later Leuyns assumed the surname of his great uncle Dr. Henry Barnard of Beverley, in accordance with his will dated 1769. This surname descended through the family until the death of Ursula Mary Florence Barnard in 1938.

In 1783 Leuyns eldest son Henry Boldero Barnard (1755-1815), succeeded to the Manor of South Cave East Hall. Shortly afterwards he purchased the nearby Manor of West Hall and the Manor of Faxfleet, thereby becoming the main landowner in South Cave. The West (or Lower) Hall Manor House was already in a very dilapidated state and was demolished in 1786. During this year the estate grounds were extended and landscaped to the north and east of East Hall.

In later years Henry turned his attention to the Manor House of East Hall. In 1802 he engaged the architect Henry Hakewill to begin work on designing and rebuilding the property in a Gothic castellated design. The work was finally completed in 1809 just six years before Henry B. Barnard's death.

The Castle was extensively altered and enlarged by his nephew Charles Edward Gee Boldero Barnard, (who had inherited the property), between 1872-75. This included the addition of the bays and entrance porches on three of the fronts. On the morning when the building work was due to be completed a fire which had been smouldering overnight in the entrance hall had caught hold, causing considerable damage to the building and contents. Together with the newly formed North Cave and District Fire Brigade many local men helped to put out the fire, forming bucket chains to the Castle pond. Work began a few months later to restore the fire-damaged areas.

The Baines Hull and East Riding Directory of 1822 first recorded that John Washington the great, great grandfather of George Washington, founder of the American Republic and the first President of the United States lived in South Cave before emigrating to America in 1657. However, this statement is almost impossible to verify since there are very few documents about the Washington family in South Cave that have survived.

There is a record in the church register of the marriage of a Henry Washington to Eleanora Harrison on the 7th October 1689 some 32 years after John had sailed for America. Henry obtained possession of East Hall Manor House and estate by marriage in 1706. Unfortunately, the exact relationship of Henry to John is in doubt since there is a gap in the parish registers covering the period 1658 to 1675.

During the 1870s local historian George G. MacTurk tried to prove the Washington connection but a Colonel Joseph Chester of Philadelphia, who had spent many years researching the Washington family history was convinced that, *"The Washingtons, of South Cave were undoubtedly members of the Washington family, from which the President sprung, but were not his immediate ancestors."*

Nevertheless, Mr. Ron Fairfax, an historian and documentary maker declared in 1989 that, following painstaking research, he had discovered actual documentary evidence to prove that John Washington actually did live in South Cave for several years before he set sail in 1657 from Hull to Virginia, North America via Europe in a ship called the *"Sea Horse"*.

Mr. Fairfax believes that South Cave is of great importance to the Washington family history and probably more so than the Washington family's two undisputed ancestral homes. These were the Old Hall, Washington, near Newcastle Upon Tyne, where the family lived in the 14th century and Sulgrave Manor, Northamptonshire, the Washington family home from the early 16th century.

Mr. Fairfax blames the unresolved dispute on academics who prefer to concentrate on the Washington family's aristocratic heritage already established in the North-East and in Northamptonshire. He would like to see a visitors' centre established in South Cave to recognise the Washington link with the area and to attract American tourists, 20,000 of whom annually visit the other two sites.

Following the death of Henry Washington in 1717 the East Hall Manor and estate was acquired by John Idell who had married Henry's daughter Anne. It was John Idell who sold it to Leuyns Boldero (later Barnard), in 1748.

The Barnard family became the most influential family in South Cave and throughout the 19th century they were the main benefactors and patrons of the church and of the schools.

Following Sophia L. Barnard's death in 1910 the Castle Estate was left to trustees to manage on behalf her invalid daughter Ursula Mary Florence Barnard the last surviving member of the Barnard family in South Cave. Ursula had lived at the Castle with her mother and then with a relative, a Miss Stuart. In 1925, however, Ursula took up permanent residence in Bournmouth.

The contents of the Castle were sold by auction in the summer of that year and in the spring of 1937 the Castle with 123 acres of land was sold to Mr. J. W. Carmichael, a co-director with his three brothers in their business R. P. Carmichael and Co. Ltd., Jewellers and Silversmiths, George Street, Hull.

In 1939 following the death of Ursula in the previous year, the remainder of the estate totalling some 2,630 acres in South Cave, North Cave, Broomfleet, Ellerker and Walkington with houses and cottages, was sold in separate lots.

Following the departure of the Carmichaels in 1946 a succession of owners ensued, among whom were the Hull Brewery Company, who in 1961 acquired the Castle and grounds and converted it into a country club. In 1970 it became a residential hotel and was later bought by Enrico and Nora Freling. They carried out a three million pound upgrading and expansion programme developing a new golfing and leisure complex at the Castle.

Cave Castle Golf Hotel is now in the ownership of Hogarth Builders who purchased it in 1994. It has 25 bedrooms, two function rooms, a 60-seat restaurant, a health club as well as an 18-hole golf course set in 150 acres of parkland.

Left, workers taking a break during work on the Castle. The Goodwill Brothers, builders and contractors were engaged by Mr. J. W. Carmichael in the late 1930s to alter, modernise and reduce the size of the Castle, which had lain empty for at least thirteen years. Much work was carried out internally which included the conversion of the drawing room into bedrooms and the removal of the library fittings to change the southwest room on the ground floor for use as the new drawing room.

During the Second World War, Cave Castle served as the Headquarters for various regiments stationed in the area. The first regiment to occupy the building was the Royal Artillery, 16th Field Regiment in late 1940. During the military occupation of the Castle the Carmichael family lived in the West Lodge. Right, soldiers from the 16th Field Regiment exercising in the grounds of the Castle.

Left, Castle Farm which during the Victorian era would have provided much of the dairy and meat needs of the inhabitants of Cave Castle. It was sold together with the remainder of the estate in 1939. Mr. Walter Curtis, the Head Gardener lived in part of the large farmhouse seen here on the right of this view.

The grounds of the East Hall Manor House only consisted of about ten acres in 1759. However, following enclosure and the purchase of nearby West Hall Manor House and its estate the grounds were extended and landscaped in 1787 by the landscape gardener William Emes. It was about this time that the road was realigned further to the south and a footpath across the park was closed. An existing pond, called the 'Canal' in 1759 was also enlarged into an irregular lake with a small island. By 1839 the Manor House which by then had been rebuilt and renamed Cave Castle had parklands and gardens occupying some sixty five acres. Within the Castle grounds is St. Helen's Well situated to the north side of the lake. At one time it was covered by an arched roof with steps down to it, but was later covered with a flat stone. The large park, as well as the kitchen gardens needed a considerable amount of attention. Taken in c.1895, the above photograph shows the bearded Mr. Walter Curtis, who until c.1920 was the Head Gardener with his staff.

This rather grand Victorian conservatory, now demolished once stood in the northern part of the Castle grounds. Not far from it was a large aviary which at one time stocked a wide variety of birds which included a number of white pheasants.

A relatively new property built almost on the site of the old 19th century conservatory in the former Castle garden grounds now houses a most unusual relic. Built into the fireplace is the foundation stone of Cave Castle which had been removed during major works between 1872-75. The present owners Mr. and Mrs. Graham Herring found the abandoned stone whilst clearing out some old greenhouses. The stone bears the Barnard name and dates. The owners contacted Arthur Credland, of Kingston upon Hull City Council Museums in 1995, who verified the stone's origins and translated the Latin inscription on it to read,

Above, neglected and lost for over a hundred years, the recently recovered foundation stone from Cave Castle now forms part of a modern fireplace!

HERRICUS B. BARNARD
Henry   B. Barnard
HAS AEDES ANNO DOM MDCCCII
This building in the year of Our Lord 1802 A.D.
INCHOAVIT ANNO MDCCCIX
was begun.   In the year 1809
PERFECIT
Completed.

A brick entrance passage would have once led into this old icehouse. Now in disuse it serves more as a garden curiosity to its new owners who now also own the Cave Castle foundation stone. In its heyday, the icehouse was an invaluable asset used for preserving meat, fish, fruit and vegetables in the days before electric refrigeration. Perishables were stored in various ways in the icehouse, which would have been filled with ice to a depth of 15-20 feet and covered with straw. Food such as sides of beef, pig, lamb or game could be hung on the walls or dome. Other smaller perishable items could be stored on tables or timber floors on the ice or alternatively they could be placed directly on the ice. During winter the servants would be given the task of gathering the supplies of ice from the Cave Castle pond which was quite an unpleasant job working in damp and freezing conditions. From the mid-19th century, it may have been filled with ice imported from America or Norway which was popular at the time because it was pure and translucent.

Below, a Notice of Sale, advertising an auction of the remainder of the Cave Castle Estate in 1939.

All Saints' Church

A church was mentioned in South Cave in the Domesday Survey of 1086 but it was rebuilt in the 13th century on the same site. However, a serious fire in about 1600 caused the north side of the 13th century church to be built yet again in 1601.

Further rebuilding and restoration took place during the 19th century and the church now consists of a chancel, nave, north aisle, south transept, south porch and embattled western tower with eight pinnacles and containing three bells dated 1676, 1742 and 1744 respectively.

The Church Registers commenced in 1558, in which year every Church was required by law to keep records of births, marriages and deaths in the parish. The records show that 1558 was in fact a time of plague, for in the winter of that year some 63 people were buried with a further 57 villagers dying in the next twelve months as the sickness persisted. It is believed that these and other victims from later plagues were buried in low lying meadows, in an area to the west of the village referred to in 1633 as "Pest Ings".

The early records were copies written in Latin on loose leaves of parchment which were eventually bound in white calf, the cost being covered by Charles E. G. Boldero Barnard during 1877. However, many leaves had been lost, damaged or mislaid beforehand. There are in fact large gaps in the register particularly during the Commonwealth period 1651-1658. A large number of entries are either inaccurate, haphazard, incomplete or wholly omitted.

Faxfleet, Weedley and Broomfleet were all part of South Cave Parish until 1861. Broomfleet had a chapel but it was difficult to reach in bad weather and coffins used to be brought to South Cave by horse drawn cart, pulled by several horses in the worst weather conditions.

A rectory was mentioned in 1120, but by 1633 it was said to be in a ruinous condition. Interestingly, a lessee of the rectory in 1536 was a Leonard Beckwith who was King Henry VIII's Commissioner for the dissolution of the monasteries in East Yorkshire.

The Pilgrimage of Grace, a Yorkshire rebellion opposing the suppression of the monasteries during the reign of King Henry VIII held organised group meetings at Beverley Westwood and at High Hunsley Beacon, Drewton. On Thursday, 12th October 1536, thousands of rebels gathered at the Beacon intending to march on York, but rumours that valuables from the dissolved priories of Haltemprice and North Ferriby were hidden at South Cave Rectory turned the crowd's attention instead to Leonard Beckwith's residence in South Cave.

It is thought that this ancient baptismal font may date back to Saxon times and could well have been in the original church.

William Stapleton, the chosen leader for this district rode down from Drewton to the rectory to find a housekeeper, a terrified priest and a gathering crowd of local people. After satisfying himself that the rumours were untrue, he reported back to the waiting pilgrims. Unfortunately, they were not convinced and effectively ransacked the rectory as well as the other properties which Beckwith owned elsewhere.

Beckwith eventually brought a case against the pilgrims at the Court of the Star Chamber in London - listing the damage and property stolen which included a fur lined coat, a pair of sheets, a blanket, 23 swine, a horse and mare, a saddle and two bowls belonging to the King - all worth £12.6s 4d.

Eventually, the revolt collapsed following the execution of several of the leaders including Robert Aske who was taken in chains and hung drawn and quartered at York. Another leader Sir Robert Constable was hanged at the entrance gates to the city of Kingston upon Hull, at Whitefriargate. Beckwith was subsequently knighted and later married the daughter of the Chief Justice of England.

Church records described the rectory, which was situated in the area to the south of East Hall, West End in 1716 as being a small dwelling, some 18 yards long by 6 yards wide, built of stone and covered in thatch. In 1786 the rectory was exchanged for a thatched cottage in Market Place together with 4 acres of land. However, by the early 19th century the Market Place rectory was described as unfit for occupation and in 1845 a new one was built in the Gothic style on the eastern side of Station Road for the Reverend Edward W. Stillingfleet. It was altered and enlarged in 1872 but was replaced in 1962 by a new rectory close by.

The 'Jobson Bread Service' is an annual memorial service which has survived since its benefactor Samuel Jobson's death in 1687. The Reverend James Victor Elliott (Vicar of All Saints' Church from 1949-1968), is pictured here in 1960 distributing loaves of white bread to some of the children of the parish among whom were Dennis Thornham, David Brown, Simon Carr, Mark Elliott, John Donkin, Ann Thornham and Vivienne Smith.

Samuel Jobson was baptized on the 16th November 1623 at All Saints' Church and became during his lifetime a man of position and wealth in South Cave. He had been a steward (an attorney) of the Manor of Faxfleet and also a steward of West Hall Manor. Following his death in March 1687 he was buried within the chancel (a privilege normally reserved for the clergy). He left five acres of land and property adjoining Brantingham Church together with some land on the west side of South Cave and Brough Road, to the poor of South Cave, for the purpose of anniversary sermons and distribution of white bread.

Jobson's land and property in Brantingham were sold in 1883 and the proceeds invested, giving the trustees of the charity a much increased income. For many years about a third of the money continued to be used for the purchase of the annual Easter gift of bread, the remainder going to provide cash gifts to the elderly and needy of the original (larger), parish of South Cave at Christmas time.

In the days of extreme poverty and hardship a loaf of white bread would have been a valuable gift for some and the "white bread" specified would be something of a luxury to people more used to poorer quality rye breads. The 'Jobson Bread Service,' held every Easter Tuesday, continues the memory of a benefactor whose Christian concern for others and practical provision has now lived on for over 300 years.

Money was also left by Mrs. Elizabeth Mary Barnard, who died on the 16th February 1872. She bequeathed £1,000 to the poor widows of South Cave, the interest to be distributed annually on the 22nd day of February, the anniversary of her late husband Henry Gee Barnard's birthday.

Older villagers remember with great fondness the annual children's flower service on Whit Sunday. A large procession of Sunday School children singing, *"Oh gather the flowers together and place them near the shrine"* led by the South Cave Subscription Silver Band would walk in pairs from the vicarage on Station Road to the church for a service in the afternoon. Eve Crisp recalls that all the girls wore pretty white frilly dresses and straw hats decorated with real flowers.

An Elizabethan chalice from All Saints' Church dated 1576 and being one of only six known pieces of silver with the old Hull hallmark was sold by the Parochial Church Council with the full consent of the diocesan authorities in March 1988. The silver-gilt cup had been on permanent display in the undercroft of York Minster because it was too valuable to keep at the church. Church warden Mr. Norman Elliott said at the time, *"The decision to sell had been a difficult one ... it seemed silly to have all that money tied up in something we couldn't use. Nobody knows where the cup came from ... it is purely secular and in no way is it a church or communion cup."*

Auctioned at Christies in London the Elizabethan chalice was sold for £35,200 and helped to raise the funds needed to build the Family Centre, which is situated at the rear of the church. The Family Centre was built by unemployed local people as part of a community programme, the project taking over five years to complete. It was officially opened by the Archbishop of York, the Most Reverend and Right Honourable John Habgood on Wednesday, 12th December 1990.

Church Hill, All Saints' Church to the left and immediately beneath it can be seen an old property part of which was formerly the Bay Horse Inn. During the early 19th century the inn was combined with a joiners shop worked by the Levitt family. It was in this joiners shop that William Clowes the great evangelist and co-founder of the Primitive Methodist movement first preached in South Cave in 1819. The front section of the Bay Horse inn was demolished c.1879 and a new frontage erected on the site. On the right of the picture is Cave Castle's West Lodge (now like the East Lodge, a Grade III listed building), built in the 1870s as a carriage gateway, with a pedestrian gate on the right hand side.

Right, Robert Ernest Ward lived on Church Hill but had his workshop on Beverley Road near the Market Place. For some 32 years he was also the secretary of the local lodge of the United Ancient Order of Druids and carried on this work until his death at the age of 79 in 1954.

R. E. Ward,

PLUMBER. GLAZIER
AND GASFITTER.

Repairs to Electric Bells and
Acetylene Gas Generators and Fittings.

Church Hill :: South Cave.

Left, taken from near the brow of Church Hill we see this unusual view of an old stone property which for many years housed Charles Brown's joinery shop. It is thought he started the business at the age of 30 years in 1855 employing three men and a boy. However, in March 1883, the business ceased following Mr. Brown's untimely death at the age of 58 years.

Right, here we see the same view taken during the mid 1880s. Charles Brown's joinery shop had been extended and altered into two cottages which up until the sale of the Cave Castle Estate in 1939 were owned by the Barnard family.

Left, looking down from Church Hill into West End which is believed to be the oldest part of the village. It is closely built up along West End and along to Pinfold. The original war memorial which was erected to commemorate those local men who lost their lives during the First World War is to the extreme left in this photograph taken c.1935.

Right, Obed Thornham, had a boot and shoemaking business in West End from c.1920 until his death in the early 1950s. He and his wife Lucy had three boys Eric, Ron and Bob. Eric and Bob had their own coal merchant businesses in the district during the 1930s-50s. Eric then went into the piggery business and his two brothers joined him later. Some 3,000 pigs were kept on their farm which consisted of about 12 acres. In 1985 after Ron and Eric had both died Ron's son Martin and his wife Sandra ran the business for a short period before it was closed and the land was later sold for house building. Named after the Thornham family, Thornham Close serves as a reminder of the family's previous occupation of this area. Below, an aerial view of the former piggery.

Left, taken in 1976, Bob Thornham with walking stick and Mr. John Spink, a part-time labourer at the Thornham piggeries.

West End

West End Farm. The Brown family were the last to occupy the farm. It was sold and renovated in 1998, with a small housing development built on its adjoining land.

Right, the young boy in the photograph taken in c.1884 is believed to be Harry "Cotty" Youngsen (1871-1948), when he served as an apprentice to Walter Digby a blacksmith in Hull. By 1909 Harry had his own forge in Water Lane, South Cave and was blacksmith there until his retirement in the 1930s.

Right, seen here in the summer of 1913 are Robert Donkin and his wife Maria outside their home, Woodbine House in Annie Med Lane. The two boys are Arthur Featherstone (left), and Frank Warcup. In 1833 Robert Sharp, the village schoolmaster wrote of it as 'Peggy Medd Lane' whilst in 1855 it was referred to as Back Lane. The lane is now known as Annie Med Lane and is named after Annie, (daughter of Peggy), who once lived in Woodbine House. She was a well known village character who lived in the house upstairs on her own but kept a number of pigs downstairs. On Sunday afternoon she would go to bed and sleep until early on Monday morning when she would rise and take her butter and eggs to market to sell. Percy Rycroft Gillatt lived here after the Donkins and established a very successful business as a builder. He had formerly been employed by the Goodwill brothers and was highly regarded in his trade. As his business expanded he took on building projects as far away as Beverley and Tickton. At the west end of the land is a garage. Many years ago it was run by Harry Jackson who would hire his charabanc for trips or for transporting goods.

In 1920 Mr. John Thomas Glew Brown (left), started a poultry farm on land to the rear of West End House. Four years later he felt obliged to sell the business to pay his father Samuel's considerable debts. Samuel was a manufacturing chemist and had to sell his own business the Ovo soap factory in Mark Street, Hull in order to meet some of his creditors. The sale by auction of some 900 birds at West End House took place on Thursday, 26th June 1924. The Nunnery Walk council estate was built in 1955 on part of the former poultry farm. In 1925 John married Ellen Waudby and went to Hailsham, Sussex to manage a poultry farm for a Captain C.C. Bell. In 1932 John and Ellen returned to her parents who lived at Wesley Farm in Church Street, South Cave. They lived at the farm until August 1935 when they rented a cottage at number 47, Church Street. John set himself up in business manufacturing pig powders from home and hawking them around the district on his bicycle which was fitted with a suitcase containing drapery which he also sold. He decided to cease this line of trading in July 1938 when he secured employment at Blackburn Aircraft Company, Brough. He retired in 1965 and died on 4th August 1973 aged 75 years. His wife Ellen died aged 86 years surviving him by 17 years.

Above, this large wooden building was built by Mr. Henry Thomas in c.1925, on land adjoining his property 'Nunnery House'. The new wooden shop was rented by tailors Richard Hornsey and son Richard, (known as Eric). Mr. Hornsey, snr. had come to South Cave in 1906 where he opened his first shop at No. 40, West End. His son left the business following the Second World War and went to work for John Brown Tailors at Beverley. Another wooden shop was built next to Mr. Hornsey's business c.1930 and was occupied by Harry Thomas and his wife Florrie who sold fish and chips. Harry also ran a barbers shop from the back of the premises for a short period. After Harry's death in 1962 the business was rented by John and Eileen Underwood who continued West End Fisheries for a further 28 years until the shop and land were sold and subsequently replaced by the Castle Mews housing development.

West End Fisheries

FOR QUALITY	OPEN:	
	Monday:	TEA
	Tuesday:	LUNCH & NIGHT
FISH & CHIPS	Wednesday:	LUNCH & TEA
	Thursday:	NIGHT
	Friday:	LUNCH & NIGHT
PIES & PEAS	Saturday:	LUNCH & NIGHT

Left, Ted Carr and his young daughter Edna standing outside their general grocery shop on Church Hill. Ted manned the petrol pumps whilst his wife Hilda ran the shop. He also kept a small piggery to the rear of the premises. The family moved to Tickton, near Beverley in 1953 when Ted purchased a considerable plot of land enabling him to build a bungalow and expand his pig farm. The shop in South Cave was sold to a relative, Hector Carr who opened it as a sweet shop seen here below left.

The two wooden shops can just been seen to the right of centre of this photograph taken during the 1940s.

West End,
South Cave. Feb 15 1932

Mr J Carr

Dr to E. CARR,

⚘ TAILOR and BREECHES MAKER. ⚘

LADIES' COATS A SPECIALITY   OWN MATERIALS MADE UP

Right, this little shop (now demolished), formerly stood very near the old Congregational Church. It had previously been a millinery shop run by Hilda Carter until her marriage to Ted Carr who opened a tailoring business there in the late 1920s. Ted had served an apprenticeship with Richard Hornsey, tailor at West End. During the early 1930s the Carr family moved to a larger property on Church Hill, which they altered to incorporate a general grocery shop.

WANTED IMMEDIATELY,

Or at Lady-day next,

A MASTER for the WORKHOUSE, at South-Cave, to instruct the Poor in some kind of Labour, such as Manufacturing Worsted, or any other Employment. A House is provided Rent Free, together with about an Acre of Ground, including an Orchard and Garden; five Guineas are allowed for Coals yearly, and two or three Cows kept at a moderate expense.

Further Particulars may be known, on application to the Overseers of the Poor of South-Cave; if by letter, post-paid.
South-Cave, Feb. 12, 1816.

Below right, South Cave once had its own workhouse at No. 42, West End, situated on the corner of Beck Lane, facing what is now known as Northfield Close. The master of the workhouse was provided with a rent free house next door at No. 40, West End. Interestingly, part of the orchard referred to in the advertisement still exists within the grounds of the former workhouse. From the 16th century, parishes had been responsible for helping the poor within their boundaries. The inmates of workhouses were intended (as the word implies), to work, but this, at least for the aged, the very young, and the mentally unsound, was not

always practicable. Nevertheless, the aim was to instill the habit of work and to encourage paupers to leave the workhouse in order to find employment within the community. This advertisement in 1816 requests specifically for a new Master of the Workhouse to be able to, "... instruct the poor in some kind of labour." Life was very hard for the inmates of these institutions and the diet was basic, usually consisting of staple foods such as bread, cheese, gruel (a kind of thin oat-meal porridge), soup, potatoes and occasional meat and bacon. In the late 18th and early 19th centuries, the sum of one pound was donated annually on behalf of the Samuel Jobson Charity of South Cave to provide a dinner for the inmates at Christmas and at Cave Fair. However, the Poor Law Amendment Act in 1834

resulted in Beverley becoming the centre of the Poor Law Union which included South Cave and 31 other villages and hamlets around the town. The aim of the new Act was to decrease the burden of the local poor rates (an assessed tax levied on property and rights), by taking all paupers into a centrally situated workhouse. The annual expenditure in South Cave for out-relief and supporting the running of the workhouse was £300-£400 between 1833-34. New welfare legislation in the early 20th century made workhouses redundant by 1930. Part of the old workhouse became William Waddington's beer shop from 1890-1908. John Carr bought the house and business c.1909 but from September 1939 rented the shop to Linsley's who continued to sell beer here until 1954.

United Reformed Church

There is a memorial stone in the United Reformed Church wall which reads, *"This Church was founded in A.D. 1662 and rebuilt in A.D. 1873."* Popular belief ascribes the formation of the Chapel to the Reverend James Bayock who is said to have been the ejected minister at South Cave in 1662 under the Act of Uniformity. This Act required the prayer book to be placed in all churches, and those who refused to comply were known as Nonconformists and ejected from their Anglican churches.

Despite this belief, there does not appear to be any evidence to support the tradition that a Presbyterian meeting house was founded in 1662, since the Reverend Bayock was not old enough to be a minister at that time, being only about 14 years of age and he did not come to South Cave until 1672.

Nevertheless, it is well documented that he bought a cottage and orchard in St. Katherine's Yard, West End in April 1700 and it was there that he built a property, which by 1718 had become licensed as a Presbyterian meeting house. It is thought that it was this structure serving as a chapel which once occupied the site of the present church. In 1873 the church was rebuilt in a Romanesque style to the designs of Samuel Musgrave of Hull. Red brick, with blue-brick dressings, was used at a total cost of £790.

In the late 18th century the minister was one Thomas Ellis. He was preaching at a time when the great Arian (unitarian) controversy was raging throughout England. Ellis was one of the many followers of the doctrine of Arius of Alexandria (4th century AD), who denied the divinity of Jesus Christ. Such ardent Arian views resulted in a dispute among his congregation which compelled him to resign in 1773. A further consequence of the dispute was that the members of the chapel decided to change from Presbyterian to Congregational. This gave them more freedom and they became largely a self-governing chapel.

The Congregational Church went on to attract a number of interesting personalities to serve as its ministers. The Reverend Seth Kelso arrived to take up his ministry at the Congregational Church in 1824 at the advanced age of 76 years and served for 4 years before he finally retired in 1828. He had previously sailed aboard the ship *"Duff"* in 1796 as a missionary to Tahiti and later to the Friendly Islands in the South Pacific Ocean before returning to England in 1800.

Other missionaries from South Cave included Charles Barff who sailed in the convict ship *"Surrey"* in 1816 to the South Sea Islands at a time when, in some island communities cannibalism was still practised. After spending many years in the Pacific Islands he died in 1866 aged 76 years whilst on a voyage to Sydney, Australia where he had hoped to settle in retirement. One of his fellow missionaries serving among the South Sea Islands was Thomas Blossom, a native of North Cave. On his retirement Thomas returned to North Cave to live and became a regular worshipper from March 1849 at this Congregational Church.

Another noteworthy minister of the church was the Reverend John Allen, (Minister from 1839-46), who in 1841 wrote a travel companion entitled *"The Stranger's Guide to Ferriby, Welton, Elloughton and South Cave."* This was for passengers using the recently opened Hull to Selby railway. Priced at about 9d. the book provided visitors to the district with an interesting guide full of historical information. The book still remains a much sought after authoritative work on these villages.

The pastorate had been shared from 1814 with the Congregational Church at Elloughton and remained so until 1877 when the church was rebuilt at Elloughton and they engaged their own resident minister. Following the departure of the Reverend R. Brotherton the South Cave church was served by the Hull and East Riding Lay Preachers' Association. The Congregational Church joined the United Reformed Church in the 1970s and is still in use as a place of worship today.

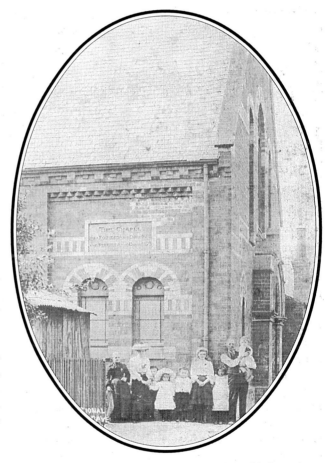

Above, an Edwardian view of the Church and left, a closer view of the foundation stone which was laid on Wednesday, 23rd April 1873 by Mr. Thomas Stratton, Vice-Chairman of the first School Board for Hull. Except for Thomas Smith & Co., slaters of Hull, all those employed to rebuild the church were local men. Mr. Thomas Goodwill was contracted as builder, Charles Brown, joiner and Mr. William Cousens, plumber and glazier. The church was officially opened on Sunday, 31st May 1874 at 2.30 p.m. with a dedicatory prayer offered by the Reverend James Sibree, of Hull. At 4 p.m. a tea was given for 375 people in the barn of Messrs. Mosey and Dunn farmers at South Cave.

Right, a view of West End looking towards Church Hill. The small white building at No. 28, West End and situated to the right of centre of this photograph was at one time Herbert Bradley's fish and chip shop. In 1930 Harry Thomas and his wife took the shop over, but after a few weeks the chimney-back collapsed and as a result they moved their business to a wooden building on Church Hill. Later Mr. Richardson, a cobbler moved into the premises and was there for many years. In 1968 he died and the shop stood empty for sometime. Fred and Florrie Gratton were the next occupants,

moving in after they had carried out substantial renovations to the property. They opened it as a newsagency also selling fruit and vegetables. Fred and Florrie retired in 1972 and the business has had a succession of different owners since then.

Left, looking towards the Pinfold, West End. From medieval times almost every village in England had its own pinfold where stray animals could be held until reclaimed by their owners. Often, they were nothing more than a small but high walled enclosure, usually rectangular, though sometimes circular. There would have also been a strong door which was kept locked. The animals remained impounded until the regulation fees were paid by the owner of the stray animal(s) to the village pinder.

George Holtby bought Smith's farm on Pinfold in 1952 moving in to farm it with his son Cecil and his son's wife Betty. Three years later Betty opened a small grocery store in part of the farm buildings, where Mr. Smith had opened a small butchers shop many years previously. In 1962 it became a self-service supermarket. In the same year Cecil bought the farm from his father and began farming it himself. As new housing developments in the vicinity grew, the shop expanded so much that by the end of the 1960s all the farm buildings had been converted into use for the shop including the barn which became a stock warehouse. Cecil stopped farming and concentrated on the shop. In 1981 the bulk of the shop was leased to Mr. Alan Shakespeare, who ran it as a 'Spar' supermarket. However, the Holtbys retained the delicatessen and butchers sections of the business for some 6 years before Alan took those over too following the Holtbys' retirement. Since the late 1980s the store has traded under the name of 'Costcutter'.

Three generations of the Jewitt family had worked and lived at Castle Farm until 1939 when the Castle Estate was sold. John Jewitt had helped in the Cave Castle laundry as well as the farm after he left school in 1921. He recalled that he would also be expected to help with the maintenance of the driveways. Often he would work on his hands and knees with eight other men in a row to pick grass and weeds out of the drives. The family moved to Elm Tree Farm built by the local Goodwill Builders on Ferry Road. Here is Doris Jewitt and Walter Donkin at their wedding reception held at No. 22, Pinfold, the home of Tommy Jewitt in 1912.

One of the earliest surviving houses in South Cave is No. 27, Pinfold, which is believed to date from about 1700 and which originally would have been thatched. Near to the Pinfold was the former site of West Hall Manor House. This property is marked on a map of 1759 as 'Mr. Richard Lloyds house', who was the Lord of the Manor. It is believed to have been built about 1175 and inhabited until 1776. It was, later demolished and the site was cleared by the end of the 18th century.

Right, built during the Second World War for military storage purposes this complex was later occupied for many years by the firm Bonhill who stored tractors and other agricultural machinery on the site. The firm closed in 1998 and the site was demolished in 1999 to make way for a new private housing development.

A little further along from the Pinfold is Ferry Road. This view looking along the road to North Cave shows to the right a row of prefabricated bungalows. Constructed shortly after the Second World War they housed ex-servicemen and their families. Harry Dennis an ex-RAF serviceman moved into one of the prefabs with his wife May and young son of 5 years. May recalls they were nicely laid out and quite spacious with a good sized garden. The dwellings were actually only meant as a temporary measure to cope with the shortage of housing at the time. Forty-six years later Harry and May finally moved out when the prefabs were all vacated for demolition in 1988. A small housing complex called The Moorlands now stands on the site.

The Hermitage

Number 42, Pinfold has been known for over one hundred years as "The Hermitage". The property is thought to have been built by Teavil Leason (1779-1865), an army captain and gentleman farmer.

A home for up to 15 inebriate women was set up by the Hull Branch of the British Women's Temperance Association in this building in July 1900. It was in fact the first such institution of its kind in the East Riding of Yorkshire. The home was opened on Thursday, 12th July in front of a large gathering of people which included Mrs. Sophia Barnard, Mr. Alfred Gelder, Mr. F. J. Reckitt and the Reverend T. J. Miller, Vicar of South Cave as well as a number of other clergymen. The opening ceremony was performed by Mrs. George H. Smith, a former Mayoress of Halifax, West Yorkshire.

The need for such a home had long been recognised by the Hull Branch of the British Women's Temperance Association. Funds raised by a series of bazaars and charitable donations had finally enabled the Association to lease The Hermitage from Mrs. Barnard of Cave Castle. It was not however, an institution to which any magistrate could commit a confirmed female alcoholic. It was run as a private home, supported partly by the income received from patients and from voluntary donations.

A minimum fee of 10 shillings was charged per patient per week, together with each individual's obligation to work. The basis upon which the home operated was that each patient contributed their labour in the interests of the home. While periods of recreation were provided it was said, " *No opportunity will be given for time to hang on the hands of the patients ... it being necessary to reclaim women from the power of strong drink.*"

Miss H. Carnie was the matron of the home. Her two assistants taught dressmaking and gardening to the patients in addition to their other caring duties. The patients were women from all the social classes and were allowed to bring their children into the home with them if necessary.

The poorest of the patients did the heavier work whilst the more affluent were given the lighter tasks in running their community home. It was described by some villagers as the place where those "Kneebrights" (a play on the word Inebriates), lived and was often a lonely place for the mothers

British Women's Temperance Association.
, HULL BRANCH.

Opening of the NEW

Home for Inebriate Women

At SOUTH CAVE.

On THURSDAY, July 12th,

The GROUNDS and HOME will be thrown

OPEN FOR INSPECTION.

TEA FROM 4-30.

Tickets, 1/- each. Afterwards a

Short Meeting will be held on the Lawn.

Chairman:

B. SMITH, Esq.

A Train leaves Cannon Street for South Cave at 1-25 returning 8-49.
Fare ONE SHILLING RETURN.

Todd, Wardell & Larter, Ltd. (R. H. Bottamley), Printers, Chapel Lane, Hull.

and an even sadder one for those children who had to live there with them.

The Hermitage continued to be used as a home for inebriate women up until c.1909. Following its closure the building was re-let by the Barnard Estate, the front section to a Mrs. Venus then later to Mrs. C. Walker and the rear portion to a Mr. C. Westbrook whose family lived there for many years. In 1939 the property was sold for £430 as part of the disposal of the Barnard Estate.

Above, after the binders have done their work, the sheaves of corn had to be stooked - that is, stood up in short double-rows so that the ears and straw could dry out in the sun and wind. Here on Common Farm are workers and young 'helpers' taking a well earned break from stooking the corn. From the right, Charlie Archer, together with his two children Wilfred and Muriel. Charlie later farmed at West Cote Farm, situated at West End, South Cave. In between the children is Willie Francis. The identity of the young man on the left-hand side of the group is unknown. The introduction of intensive farming methods in the second half of the 20th century has seen many of the traditional tasks such as stooking taken over by combine harvest machines. With one of these machines the corn can be cut and threshed in one operation. Common Farm lies about one mile south west of West End and together with nearby Mill Farm is one of several outlying post-enclosure farmhouses in South Cave which were built on low ground southwest of the village. Mill Farm stands near the site of a former water-mill which was known as Low (or West), Mill. A water-mill was recorded as being in use there as far back as 1391. The farm and mill were rebuilt in 1857, although, it appears that the water-mill was no longer in use by the end of the 1860s.

Farmer George Collins of Common Farm with his new binder c.1905. These machines became more common towards the end of the 19th century. The operator rode on a seat fixed at the rear-end while usually two pairs of horses were yoked tandem fashion to the front. Understandably, farmers quickly took to using these strange looking contraptions since these were the first models of the combined harvester and were able in one operation to cut the corn, pack and tie it into sheaves. As a consequence the farmers' labouring costs were reduced as the number of harvesters needed fell accordingly. Further mechanisation and the progressive introduction of tractors after the end of the First World War saw additional reductions both in the labour force and the use of horses on the land.

Cave Fair

From at least the 13th century there is evidence that regular weekly markets were held in South Cave for the sale of farm and dairy produce, game, poultry and farm animals. In 1840 the market declined shortly after the opening of the Hull to Selby Railway, when much larger markets in the West Riding of Yorkshire became more easily accessible.

In about 1870 an attempt was made to revive the market but it only lasted for some three months despite no tolls (rent) being charged and the free use of the Market Hall.

South Cave also once boasted two fairs a year before it lost much of its importance as a market town. The first annual fair was held over four days during the feast of Holy Trinity (a moveable Christian church festival designated the Sunday following Whit Sunday in honour of the Holy Trinity) and the second in October usually on the second Monday after Michaelmas Day (29th September).

Whilst the trading of livestock was taking place during Trinity week there were sports, feasts and pleasure fairs which the whole district shared. On Monday the pleasure fair began in North Cave and for a number of years it included horse racing at Crosslands Lane. On Tuesday the festivities moved to South Cave and on Wednesday the entertainments moved to Ellerker. On Thursday it was Newport Feast and Broomfleet fair on Saturday.

Trinity Sunday was known as Cave Fair Sunday and housewives celebrated by making dozens of cheesecakes or 'chissocks' in preparation for the large influx of friends and relatives who were accommodated for the celebrations.

By the 1890s the Trinity Fair was largely for pleasure and it survived into the 1940s. From 1937 the pleasure fair was started on Saturday instead of Tuesday and continued until Wednesday night. There were stalls all along the Market Place and merry-go-rounds, swings and other attractions were set up in Fair Field, the first small field on the south side of Beverley Road.

The October fair was a horse, sheep and cattle fair and was first held on Monday, 24th October 1831. Up until the introduction of the Hull and Selby Railway in 1840, farmers would regularly bring their livestock from as far away as North Lincolnshire on the ferry via Wintringham and Brough.

Although this annual Monday fair was still in existence in 1920 it had ceased altogether by 1925. Archie Trout the South Cave historian mentions in his diary for Tuesday, 12th October 1920 that the fair had been held on that day, a day later than usual in order to avoid occurring on the same day as the opening of Hull Fair.

Despite this rearrangement of the event Archie commented, *"The whole countryside, almost, went to town this day, crowded trains of farmers, farmhands and company."*

It would appear that competing with the annual Hull Fair in October had eventually resulted in the demise of the South Cave horse, sheep and cattle fair a few short years later.

Above, North Cave Sports in Fairfield, Station Road held on the 15th July 1909. Below, the three winning entries for the 'Best Decorated Bicycle' event and to the left a table laden with prizes awaiting the winners of the various competitions.

In 1909 it was decided as part of the North Cave Show to revive the Horse and Foal Show, which had not been held since 1897. It was strongly supported by the local gentry, Colonel J. B. Stracey-Clitherow was elected president and Mr. T. S. Whitaker of Everthorpe Hall, vice-president. Some £80 was offered in prize money and the event attracted a huge number of entries. Above, one of the first prize winners with his yearling, beautifully decorated and groomed for the occasion.

Brothers, Hedley (left) and Gordon Cousens with the enormous array of prizes won between them at various village sports days. This photograph was taken in April 1913 in the back garden of their home 'Chestnut Villa' number 26, Church Street, South Cave. Hedley Close in the West End of the village was named after Hedley who had owned property and land there.

The traditional annual village sports held on South Cave Fair Day during Trinity week survived until the Second World War. Although an attempt was made to revive it in 1951 the event was not particularly successful and it was the last to be held.

The annual sports day was held successively on the old cricket field at the back of Wesley Farm, Church Street and then later on the old football field near Cow Pasture. At the height of its popularity, everyone was charged an entrance fee into the sports field and competitors had to pay an additional fee to enter each event. This money as well as general fund-raising and donations contributed by villagers, helped to finance the occasion and pay for prizes.

The open races brought in keen competitors from far afield. The mile race attracted the most entries. Local people took part in the fancy dress, tug of war, sack races, egg and spoon races and the married men's three legged races. There were also plenty of children's running, skipping, obstacle and hopping races throughout the day. In some years there were more unusual events such as a novelty 6 a-side football match on cycles. Although it cost 3/- per team to enter, the first prize was 7/- for each player. Another year motor cycle musical chairs was tried with lady pillion riders.

The pleasure fairs are remembered with great fondness by older inhabitants. In South Cave there were stalls all along Market Place and for many years fair ground operators such as Corrigans would set up roundabouts and swings in Fair Field at the rear of Market Place Farm.

Each year new novelty articles would be on sale. These are known to have included "squirts" which were metal tubes, the size of large toothpaste tubes, filled with water. Youths bought them deriving their pleasure by parading around the field shooting out the water into girls' faces. Another time, tickling brushes were the innovation. Each had a handle of twisted wire about a foot long with a tassel-like bunch of coloured yarn at the end. Again they attracted the boys who tickled the faces of any females they met. Very tasty and popular were the hot mushy peas which were sold on small saucers by an enterprising man from Ellerker.

The traditional Cave Fair Cheesecakes were made especially for the occasion. Although cheesecakes were common all year round, the pastry was made richer and the curd often made of new milk instead of old and an extra egg would be added. Everyone made cheesecakes and they all went round sampling each others; there seemed to be an endless amount of recipes as well as cooks.

SOUTH CAVE FAIR 1951

SPORTS

to be held in the Castle Grounds (by kind permission of T. F. Dodsworth, Esq.)
(Entrance W.I. Hut, Church Street)

on

TUESDAY, MAY 22nd,

(Weather Permitting)

Commencing at 6-0 p.m.

ADMISSION: - ADULTS 1/6; CHILDREN 6d.

Programme—Sixpence

OFFICIALS

Referee—Mr. W. Goodwill
Judges—Rev. T. V. Elliott, Mr. R. G. Harris
Starter—Mr. T. H. Smith
Handicapper—Mr. Nothard
Announcer—Mr. J. K. Byrne
Committee—Messrs. W. S. Brumfield (Chairman), N. Calvert, W. Donkin, P. Gillett, F. Gillett, L. Hurd, F. Jude, W. Jewitt, A. Moverley, D. Platt, T. H. Smith, A. Taylor, H. Thomas, B. Thornham, J. Wiseman
Hon. Secretary—A. S. Daniel
Hon. Treasurer—H. Sutcliffe

Holroyd & Asquith, Printers, Dunns Lane, Howden Tel. 361

Bostock and Wombwell's Travelling Menagerie and Circus

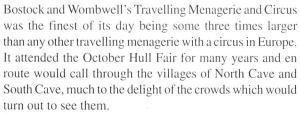

One of Bostock's elephants seen here at Wesley Farm, South Cave c.1925.

Bostock and Wombwell's Travelling Menagerie and Circus was the finest of its day being some three times larger than any other travelling menagerie with a circus in Europe. It attended the October Hull Fair for many years and en route would call through the villages of North Cave and South Cave, much to the delight of the crowds which would turn out to see them.

Before photography became more popular and the invention of television the sight of strange live animals was a huge attraction. Year after year came the show vans containing the savage caged lions, tigers, leopards, panthers, jaguars, hyenas, wolves, bears as well as a wagon full of monkeys. Walking along with their trainers would be the camels, lamas and the lumbering elephants.

The menagerie always stopped at Newport Canal to wash down the animals and then in James Anderson's (the village blacksmith) field near Townend Bridge at North Cave where they would stop overnight while he worked day and night to shoe the horses. The local beck was also useful for providing drinking water for the animals.

Sometimes the show tent would be erected and locals would pay 3d. to watch the clowns, acrobats, jugglers and horse riders as well as the performing dogs and elephants. Alf Adamson of Hotham remembers going to see the show as a young boy. One thing that stood out in his memory was a clown who borrowed a handkerchief from one of the spectators, made it into a doll by folding it, then put it on the ground and told it to dance - which it did. Alf never understood how the clown did it.

At South Cave too the tent would sometimes be raised and the locals treated to a show. Usually, it was erected in a field at Wesley Farm (now demolished), in Church Street. The performances were for one day only and there was star billing given to at least one particular animal in the hope of attracting as many people as possible to the show.

In some years for example it would be a performing polar bear, or a boxing kangaroo or even an extraordinary zoological novelty such as a hybrid, half lion, half tiger.

Right, an advertisement for the Hull Fair in October 1902, which promises an appearance by Wallace the Veteran Lion as well as a host of other animal attractions.

Above, Wallace was billed as 'The Untamable Lion' . He was said by Bostock and Wombwell to have been responsible for killing Captain Omgoso, a reknown lion tamer. This lion was the main attraction of the menagerie in the mid 1890s and he is seen here in his cage which doesn't appear to be too secure! One of the highlights of the show in 1895 was when his trainer Martini Barthert placed his head into the lion's mouth. It is probably no coincidence that in Marriott Edgar's famous monologue, the lion who ate Albert was called Wallace.

BOSTOCK AND WOMBWELL'S

ROYAL No. 1 AGGREGATION,

The Most Complete and Up-to-Date Travelling Menagerie ever seen,

WILL VISIT HULL FAIR FROM OCTOBER 10th TILL OCTOBER 16th, ON THE FAIR GROUND.

MORE VALUE THAN EVER. FRESH ATTRACTIONS. STARTLING PERFORMANCES.

Besides the 700 BIRDS, BEASTS, and REPTILES, and the 7 DISTINCT GROUPS OF PERFORMING LIONS, TIGERS, LEOPARDS, PUMAS, BEARS, and WOLVES, amongst them being the Veteran Lion "WALLACE," we have just added the following interesting NOVELTIES, which are to be seen FREE OF ANY EXTRA CHARGE during our visit to this town:—WILD BOARS FROM WINDSOR PARK, presented to Mr Bostock by His Majesty the King; THE BELL-RINGING MAFEKING MONKEY; GIANT AND MIDGET HORSES; GIANT AND MIDGET DONKEYS; The Transvaal Wonder, THE HAIRLESS MARE; and last, but not least, the King of all Equine Novelties—"WHITE WINGS," the Long-maned and Tailed Horse. A beautiful White Horse, with Mane and Tail measuring 40 feet. Value £1,000.

No one should miss seeing the Show on its present visit; in fact, do not fail to witness it enter your town, and that will give you some idea of its extensive nature.

PERFORMANCES FROM 12 NOON UNTIL 10.30 P.M.

ADMISSION SIXPENCE; CHILDREN HALF-PRICE.

Proprietor: E. H. BOSTOCK, The Scottish Zoo, Glasgow.

Manager in Person: H. F. BIRKETT.

In 1904 the South Cave Subscription Brass Band was formed and all the instruments were purchased second hand. The Band was invariably in attendance at the local village fairs, playing a selection of popular melodies throughout the day. Initially, practice nights were held in a room in the Town Hall. However, following complaints in the early 1920s from members of the Parish Council who shared the premises and who noted in their records that, "... exception was taken to the noisy and unseemly conduct of some of the younger members of the Band ...," the practice sessions were consequently moved to a hut at the rear of the Bear Inn public house in the Market Place. In 1925 owing to the poor state of the instruments, the committee decided to form a new Silver Band. Over the following two years all engagement fees (excepting actual expenses) and the members annual subscriptions of 8s. 8d. funded the £400 needed to purchase the new uniforms and new Class A silver plated instruments. Above left inset, Fred Moore, (1895-1958), saddler and shoemaker, of Church Street was the Bandmaster from 1920-1931. Here we see the Band before the new Silver Band was formed. Below right inset, Arthur Smith, (1885-1956), Butcher of Church Street was the succeeding Bandmaster until the Band's demise in 1938 prior to the commencement of the Second World War when many of the players were called up to serve in the forces. The uniforms and instruments were later sold and the money was used to buy a large number of laurel bushes which were planted around the village. Below, the South Cave Subscription Silver Band in 1931 in their new uniforms and with their new instruments.

Memories of the 1935 Silver Jubilee, 1937 Coronation and 1953 Coronation Celebrations

Coronations and Jubilees were occasions for much celebration by local communities in the days before television became a main source of entertainment. These events were looked upon as an opportunity to encourage as many people in the village as possible to take part in the proceedings. Various committees were formed many months in advance to organise and discuss the programme for each particular occasion.

North Cave and Hotham of course celebrated such events with as much enthusiasm as South Cave. For example, as well as dances and whist drives, a tea-party for over 1,000 people was organised and served by the local Women's Institute in Hotham Park during May 1935 in order to celebrate the Silver Jubilee of King George V and Queen Mary.

It is unfortunate that hardly any photographs survive to record these efforts. As a consequence the following few pages show mainly South Cave's celebrations. Nevertheless, they illustrate the patriotic fervour that was common in all villages and which certainly came to the fore during the 1935 Silver Jubilee event, the Coronation of King George VI in 1937 as well as the 1953 Coronation of Queen Elizabeth II.

Right, taking part in the 1935 Jubilee Pageant of Fashion and Transport was Miss Fanny Carr riding in a carefully crafted rickshaw on pram wheels. The rickshaw is seen here passing L. B. Walker's shop in the Market Place being pulled by a willing servant.

Above, James Freeman re-enacting the part of the inn keeper of the old Windmill inn, Market Place with daughter Minnie Freeman as a serving wench. The group is passing Wesley Farm, (now demolished), in Church Street.

In 1935 to commemorate the Silver Jubilee of King George V and Queen Mary the clock tower was illuminated by public subscription and a plaque erected within the entrance to South Cave Town Hall. The day was celebrated with an opening re-enactment of the granting of the Charter to South Cave c.1330 which took place on the steps of the Town Hall. About seventy local villagers took part in The Pageant of Fashion and Transport that followed. The main character was Dick Turpin played by Mr. Alan Hall, who re-enacted the infamous highwayman's escape from the law by riding his horse Black Bess through the village, calling in briefly to have his horse reshod at the old Windmill Inn, which had been specially reopened for the occasion. The South Cave Subscription Silver Band played at the head of the Jubilee procession to the Cave Castle grounds where the following events took place:- Sports races, baby show, decorated bicycles, decorated perambulators and fancy dress. Mrs. Walter Waudby presented the prizes. The sports prizes were presented by Dr. and Mrs. G. Thompson. Prizes were also given for the best decorated houses and were won by Mr. Freeman of Market Place, Mrs. Moat of Market Place and Mr. B. Waudby of Church Street. In the evening a dance was held in the Women's Institute hut in Church Street. During the evening a bonfire was lit at Mount Airy and rockets set off at 10 p.m. Tea was served throughout the day in all the available buildings in the village.

When King George V died in 1936 his eldest son, who inherited the Crown as King Edward VIII chose instead to abdicate in order to marry his close companion Mrs. Wallis Simpson an American divorcee. His successor was his brother Albert, Duke of York, who took the title of King George VI. The nation celebrated his Coronation with much happiness on Wednesday, 12th May 1937. Due to the inclement weather both the North Cave and South Cave Coronation Pageants were delayed until Cave Fair day, held for the first time on a Saturday instead of Tuesday. At Hotham the Coronation events went ahead as planned, beginning with sports for the children. Each child then received sweets, oranges, ice-cream and a Coronation mug followed by tea for all the locals in the village. Also, a social and dance was held in the evening. The South Cave Coronation Pageant is vividly remembered for the range of costumes and themes which were very inventive. First in the procession, which began at the southern end of the Market Place, came the 'Nursery Rhymes' followed by characters from legends. Above, the Pied Piper played by Fred Moore together with the citizens of Hamelin halted at the reopened Windmill Inn, Market Place where the story was re-enacted, as was also the story of Old King Cole with his fiddler's three. Ben Taylor who was one of the fiddlers recalled that the King was played by Tommy Cole. Then came the 'Peoples of the Empire' ranging from a Sultan and his harem, to a tribe of Zulu warriors. The procession was reformed at the northern end of the Market Place where it marched down into Church Street and then along to Cave Castle. Mr. Walter Waudby was the Chairman of the Pageant Committee, Mr. J. W. Hickson was the pageant producer and Mr. G. F. Beecham Hall (Headmaster of the Boys' School), was the commentator. In the Castle grounds there was a fancy dress parade for children, motor and horse-drawn vehicles on show and a bowls competition. In the evening a programme of sports took place and a fancy dress carnival dance was held in the Church Institute. The day concluded with a huge bonfire and fireworks on Mount Airy.

A tribe of local Zulu warriors! As part of the 1937 Coronation Pageants historical theme these costumes would have been worn to commemorate the Anglo-Zulu War of 1879, which was one of Britain's bloodiest colonial wars and had taken place only some 58 years previously.

Many of the village children took part in the 1937 pageant dressed as characters from nursery rhymes. Above, the fancy dress procession pauses for a photo-call. Below right, the procession heading northwards through the Market Place.

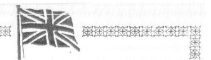

During the 1953 Coronation Year the British Legion Flower, Fruit and Vegetable Show was held in Mr. Tom Gibson's workshop in Church Street, pictured above. In the early 1960s the workshop was incorporated into Gibson's Garage and was finally demolished c.1982.

Edna Copeland (nee Thomas), as Queen Elizabeth II is seated in the centre of the Royal float. Her other regal companions were, front left, Peggy Charlton as Queen Ann, right, Amy Smith as Queen Elizabeth I. Back left, Nancy Brumfield as Queen Victoria, right, Phyllis Sutcliffe as Queen Mary. The chauffeur driving the tractor is Harold Young. This photograph was taken as the float was passing the old Girls' School in Church Street.

In spite of biting winds, rain showers and grey skies the village celebrations for the Coronation of Queen Elizabeth II on Tuesday, 2nd June 1953, carried on regardless. The streets of South Cave were lined with crowds and bunting and all the events went ahead as planned except for the sports activities which were postponed until the Saturday of that week.

The highlight of the day was a procession led by Mrs. B. Kiff as Britannia, followed by an enthroned Queen Elizabeth II, surrounded on each corner of the float by four previous Queens. The tableaux and vehicles, which included decorated bicycles and preambulators assembled in Mr. George Arthur Hall's stackyard at Parkside Farm, Church Street and proceeded via Back Lane, Market Place and West End returning to the Recreation Ground.

At the end of the procession Queen Elizabeth II played by Edna Copeland alighted from her carriage and was crowned by the "Archbishop of Canterbury" acted by the Reverend James V. Elliott. Souvenir mugs were presented by Mrs. Nancy Brumfield from the steps of the Town Hall to all the children. A children's tea was given two days later followed by a programme of films, including a free ice-cream, in the local cinema in Church Street.

On the evening of the 2nd June, adults enjoyed a free whist drive followed by a dance in the Women's Institute. On the stroke of 10.00 p.m. that evening a huge beacon was fired on Mount Airy which was accompanied by a display of rockets. Simultaneously, with the lighting of the fire the reinstalled floodlighting of the Town Hall clock was switched on by the Chairman of the Parish Council, Mr. Walter S. Brumfield.

The crowning of Queen Elizabeth II of South Cave. The Reverend Elliott taking his part as Archbishop of Canterbury very seriously much to the amusement of Edna Copeland who took the part of the Queen. Edna was chosen for the role by one of the organisers of the event, Mrs. Nancy Brumfield, who thought she bore quite a close resemblance to the actual Queen Elizabeth II.

At North Cave the celebrations began at 10 a.m. with an Open-Air Service of Thanksgiving at "The Croft," home of Colonel William Henton Carver followed by the presentation of Souvenir Mugs to all children under 15 years of age. In the afternoon the crowning of the village Coronation Queen Miss C. Waudby took place on the steps of the War Memorial on Station Road. Shortly afterwards competitors in the fancy dress parade were transported on floats from the War Memorial down Westgate to Townend Bridge, Low Lane, Nordham, Blossom Lane up to Church Street. Right, the

procession passing the old wooden fish and chip shop in Church Street, to Hotham Park where a Coronation tea had been organised by the North Cave Women's Institute for all residents of North Cave and Hotham. Those who wished to attend the tea were requested to bring their own cups and cutlery! A door-to-door collection was organised to raise funds to pay for this public tea and social event. A sports evening was also organised for adults in Hotham Park which included such events as the popular 100 yards flat race for men, a wheelbarrow race, three-legged race for ladies and gentlemen and a horse race. At the end of the evening, there were fireworks and a bonfire in the park combined with community singing and dancing. The celebrations continued on the Saturday with children's sports and in the evening a comic cricket match was held in the Park and was organised by North Cave Cricket Club.

Right, members of the South Cave Youth Club dressed as a tribe of Red Indians. Cynthia May is dressed as a rather convincing squaw in the foreground.

Left, part of the Coronation fancy dress procession passing the Bear Inn Market Place.

The floats portrayed a wide range of themes, for example a John Wesley scene, a film scene from Alice in Wonderland and a very realistic pirates' ship complete with a wicked looking crew. Above, local children portray a scene from the Mad Hatter's Tea Party from Alice in Wonderland. Below, a group of Dutch bulb field workers are portrayed complete with a windmill and tulips. These photographs are reproduced by courtesy of Innes Photographers tel: 01482-649271.

The War Years

The First World War

In the Bosnian city of Sarajevo on the morning of Sunday, 28th June 1914, while on a routine visit, Archduke Franz Ferdinand of Austria, a nephew and heir of the Austro-Hungarian Emperor, and his wife, were assassinated by a Bosnian student. This event was the catalyst for the start of the First World War - the Great War - in which ten million men died and another twenty million were wounded.

With the outbreak of hostilities the British Government recognised that this country's armed forces would have to be greatly increased if Britain and its allies were to win the war. Lord Kitchener, the newly appointed War Minister issued a call for 100,000 men on the 14th August 1914 and further calls followed. Within a year over two million men had volunteered nationwide.

In each county Volunteer Regiments were formed under the auspices of their respective Lord Lieutenants. Each Lord Lieutenant appointed an officer known as the County Commandant who took responsibility for all the administration, organisation and discipline of all Volunteers in his county. For the East Riding of Yorkshire Colonel W. Lambert White was selected for this post.

In 1914 the East Yorkshire Regiment consisted of five battalions but by the end of that year seven additional battalions had been formed for the new armies of Lord Kitchener. Never, in the history of the Regiment, had recruits joined in such numbers and at such a rapid pace, clearly answering the call to arms.

Early in 1915 the formation of the 3rd or County Battalion was approved for recruiting and training Volunteers from the whole of the East Riding of Yorkshire outside the Kingston upon Hull City boundaries. The task of raising and establishing the Battalion was entrusted to Lieutenant Colonel J. B. Stracey-Clitherow of Hotham Hall, Hotham. The headquarters were formed at the Yeomanry Offices, Railway Street, Beverley, in the first instance but were shortly afterwards moved to larger premises at the Territorial Barracks, Grayburn Lane, Beverley.

The Lord Lieutenant, recognising the threat of east coast attacks by the Germans, appealed for donations from organisations and businesses. The Kingston upon Hull City Corporation and the East Riding County Council each donated £1,000 thereby contributing to an aggregate total of £17,600 which was spent on the purchase of arms, equipment and clothing.

Within a short period the 3rd Battalion was also armed with 2,800 Martini-Henry Rifles and 100,000 rounds of ammunition and kitted out in grey-green cloth uniforms. The Battalion was thought to have been ahead of any other in the country at this time since most volunteers were drilling with wooden rifles and clad in cotton makeshift uniforms.

The volunteers, as well as patrolling the east coast line, undertook a range of duties including guarding munition works, lines of railways, bridges and other vulnerable points in East

The Lord Lieutenant of East Yorkshire, Lord Nunburnholme was requested by the War Office to persuade as many men as possible from the city of Kingston upon Hull and the East Riding of Yorkshire to volunteer as soldiers. He made strong appeals to the patriotism of the public and as a consequence recruits came forward in large numbers. Thousands of men were recruited from the city and village after village offered sections or platoons when the East Yorkshire Volunteer Brigade, (3rd or County Battalion), was established.

Yorkshire. Despite the huge numbers of volunteers locally and nationwide, conscription had to be introduced in March 1916 to replace the appalling losses suffered in trench warfare during the preceeding two years. The 3rd. Battalion carried on drafting, equipping and training men to replace those killed and wounded in the regular and service battalions.

In December 1916, it was decided to form a new 4th Battalion, the nucleus of which was to be two of the Companies of the 3rd Battalion. Officers and men who transferred from the 3rd Battalion included the "B" Company, commanded by Captain F. Linsley, which had detachments at South Cave, North Cave, Hotham, Welton, Hessle and Cottingham.

The Headquarters for the "B" Company were based at Cottingham where basic training was given and included courses in musketry, bombing, hotchkiss gun, anti-gas, bayonet-fighting, cookery and signalling. It is worthy of record that in the four years of the existence of the 3rd and 4th Battalions, some 15,600 men passed through on their way to the battle front in France and the port of Salonika in Greece which the Allies intended to use as a base for campaigns to aid Serbia.

These photographs taken in 1915 are of the 1st East Yorkshire Brigade Supply and Transport Corps in Market Place, South Cave. This unit was raised by the Sheriff of Kingston upon Hull, Sir Erick Ohrson and it had the distinction of being the only Horse Transport Company formed in the United Kingdom. Here, soldiers from the unit are commandeering horses and carts from the area. The local vet Challenger Alcock and Joseph Foster, landlord from The Albion Inn, North Cave, (who was also a horse-breaker), helped to locate and examine suitable horses for collection.

Here in the yard at the rear of Market Place Farm are a number of local horses ready to be taken away for war-service. Known as 'Remounts' they were used to replace horses which had been killed or wounded abroad.

Archie Trout, the South Cave historian kept a diary throughout the First World War. In it he recorded that he had been rejected from military service on medical grounds. Carrying on working full time as a Collector of Accounts for the London North Western Railway in Hull he spent much of his spare time assisting in war work and charities at home.

His wife's brother Harold Dixon regularly wrote letters from the trenches. These included a few pages written from the Somme battlefield and from which Archie recorded extracts in his diary. On one occasion Harold wrote that out of a group of one hundred and fifteen men who had been in the trenches of the Somme, only twelve had returned, nine of whom had gone straight into hospital. He also reported about a new British invention called a 'tank' which he described as having, "... caterpillar wheels and can drive right over the trenches, spitting fire from guns as they go and dragging up any barbed wire that happens to be in their way."

One charity committee that Archie helped to organise was the South Cave Soldiers Christmas Parcels Committee. The idea was to send parcels to local soldiers serving in the forces. Each parcel had a value of about 8 shillings and contained a pair of socks, 50 cigarettes, a pocket diary, writing pad, tablet of coal-tar soap and other items which were given by villagers on 'Gift Day'.

Some 100 parcels were dispatched to those serving overseas in December 1916. Eighty four replies had been received by late January 1917 from servicemen expressing their gratitude. Although the annual Cave Fair had been suspended for the duration of the war the traditional baking of cheesecakes went ahead in June 1916 and dozens of them were sent to local boys serving on the front line.

From June 1915 the war had been brought a lot closer to home with air-raids affecting many major cities including Hull. Early on Wednesday, 9th August 1916 there were up to ten Zeppelins dropping bombs over the north east coast. One of the airships was clearly observed flying over North Cave and at West End, South Cave. As a result many households blacked out their windows at night as a precaution against the night time air raids.

Defending the Humber area was the responsibility of No. 33 Squadron and a field to the northwest of South Cave was brought into use as a night landing air strip. After the war it fell into disuse and there is no longer any trace left of it today.

The First World War ended with the signing of the Armistice on the eleventh hour of the eleventh day of the eleventh month, 1918. Although there was much celebration throughout the nation the war had resulted in over 30 million casualties world wide and one in ten of this country's young men had been killed with many more wounded or maimed.

In spite of the Armistice, war was still considered a distinct possibility right up until the signing of the peace treaty in July 1919 and therefore demobilisation was much delayed. On Saturday, 19th July 1919 many towns and villages throughout the country conducted their own peace celebrations.

In Hull, there was a procession which included the Army and Navy units, volunteers, boys' and girls' organisations, decorated rullies and cycles, and numerous bands. At South Cave a tea was given for all inhabitants in Cave Castle Park. Sports events were held in the football field and later there was a firework display finishing with a bonfire on Beverley Clump at 11 p.m.

On the first anniversary of Armistice Day at 11.a.m. on Tuesday, 11th November Archie Trout wrote, "The wheels of traffic stood still throughout the British Isles and there was a 'Great Silence' in memory of the gallant dead. Men stood with their heads bared, traffic was silent for two minutes."

During the evening of the same day a "Welcome Home" gathering took place in South Cave with over one hundred returned soldiers present. A three course supper was given followed by a concert programme. For those local men who had tragically lost their lives memorials were later erected by public subscription in their respective villages.

This rather poignant poem was penned by an unknown local man and recited in the former Albion Hotel in order to raise money for the Red Cross Funds during the First World War. Joe Foster was the landlord and is referred to in the poem. Nineteen local men lost their lives in the war and their names are commemorated on the war memorial which was erected on Stocks Hill at the village end of Station Road.

The Lads From North Cave

"England is in danger," says the posters on
the wall
There's lots of lads I know right well who
have answered England's call
Some have left their parents, their children
and their wives
To go to fight for England and sacrifice their
lives
There is now a dozen lads I know quite well
Who patronise the dramship at the Albion Hotel
They swore they would do their bit, their
country to save
And prove themselves a credit to the village
of North Cave
Wherever there was danger they never saw fear
They could fight, die for England and
Bentley's Yorkshire Beer
Some they like to stay at home and papers read
each night
But the good old lads belonging Cave, would
rather go and fight
F. H. G. first took the lead and to the
sergeant went
Several more then followed for on listing they
were bent
All but one then noted and he is not to blame
The one I refer to Joe Foster is his name
No doubt he would like to go and fight for
England dear
But his duty is to stay at home supplying
Bentley's Beer
And when the lads they do return at the finish
of the fight
We'll all meet at the Albion and have a
glorious night
We know they have done their bit their country
for to save
has these gallant lads of Yorkshire from the
village of North Cave.

Children from the North Cave village schools are being marched by their teachers to the unveiling ceremony of the war memorial. The girls wore white dresses, whilst the boys wore sailor suits.

The North Cave memorial was designed by a London architect Mr. Temple Moore and was built and erected by Ullathornes of Selby. The unveiling ceremony took place on Saturday, 25th June 1921 in the presence of a huge crowd. The proceedings opened with the singing of the hymn, "Ten thousand times ten thousand, In sparkling raiment bright" accompanied by Mr. Tom Denton, organist of All Saints' Church on a harmonium. The lesson was read by the Reverend Vipond Byles, Wesleyan Minister and the prayers of thanksgiving were conducted by the Reverend John W. Graham. The Primitive Methodist Minister Reverend M. N. Rice dedicated the memorial and read out the names of the war dead. Miss Patricia Carver, in unveiling the memorial said, "I unveil this memorial to the Glory of God and in ever grateful memory of the men of North Cave who gave their lives in the Great War." The service was closed by the singing of the national anthem.

The bedecked village hall in Westgate, in readiness for the start of the welcome home celebrations upon the return of some of its more fortunate soldiers from the First World War.

The South Cave Service of Dedication of the War Memorial was held on Saturday, 13th August 1921 at 4 p.m. The memorial in the shape of a large tall white cross was erected in front of West Lodge, West End, South Cave and was unveiled by Colonel B. G. Price, C. B; C. M. G; D. S. O. Commandant of the York and Durham Brigade. The ministers taking part were the vicar of All Saints' Church the Reverend John William Graham, the Primitive Methodist Circuit Minister and the Wesleyan Circuit Minister, Mr. Eastwood. The South Cave Subscription Silver Band took part as did the "Comrades", soldiers who had served in the Great War. Unfortunately, the war memorial cross was subject to much maintenance and many repairs, and on several occasions large pieces of stone broke away rendering it a danger to the general public. As a consequence, within 4 decades the structure was demolished. Following a public meeting in November 1958 a much smaller memorial was placed on the same site.

Right, the small village of Hotham also erected a war memorial to remember their six soldiers who had lost their lives in the First World War. It was officially unveiled on Monday, 24th May 1920. Seven Burn brothers brought up in a property known as" The Bungalow" in the village served in the war. Five of them survived but Charles and Albert were killed. Private Charles Burn, serving in the Army Reserve when war was declared, went out with the first expeditionary force and fought in the Battle of Mons, where he was wounded and later died from his injuries. His parents received the "Mons Star" medal awarded to him posthumously. A notice was received by the Parish Council on the 25th November, 1942 stating that the railings which surrounded the memorial were to be requisitioned for the Second World War effort. They were subsequently melted down for recycling but were never replaced owing to the expense.

Still on the gates of the Town Hall, Market Place, South Cave is a wooden memorial tablet which records the names of the men from the area who fell in the Great War. On "Comrades National Memorial Day," members of the local Old Comrades Association would march from the vicarage on Station Road, with the South Cave Subscription Silver Band at their head, to this memorial, where the vicar, the Wesleyan preacher and several Comrades would conduct a service. Hymns were sung and a wreath placed on the memorial. Afterwards the procession went down to the Parish Church for an indoor service.

-⊦- FORM OF SERVICE -⊦-

ON THE OCCASION OF THE

Dedication of the Memorial

AT HOTHAM,

Erected in honour of the men who served
in the Great War, 1914—1918.

AND TO BE

Unveiled by Mrs. T. Gurney,

OF HOTHAM HALL,

ON WHIT-MONDAY (EMPIRE DAY),

MAY 24TH, 1920.

AT 3.0 P.M.

The Second World War

At precisely 11.15 a.m. on Sunday, 3rd September 1939, the B.B.C. wireless programmes were interrupted for a broadcast by the Prime Minister, Neville Chamberlain. He announced that Hitler had not replied to the British Government's final ultimatum sent two-and-a-quarter hours earlier and that Britain and Germany were therefore at war.

While the Second World War was to have devastating effects in terms of destruction on the city of Kingston upon Hull some 15 miles away, South Cave, North Cave and the surrounding villages remained comparatively unscathed.

However, the war brought many changes. While most of the local young men were conscripted into the forces, newcomers such as soldiers, evacuees and prisoners of war were billeted in the area. In addition new groups sprang up from the Civil Defence Movement such as the Woman's Voluntary Service, Air Raid Patrol Wardens, Auxiliary Fire Service and the Home Guard.

Like everywhere else in the country, small communities were constantly asked to help organise events and contribute in any way they could in order to aid the war effort. The following few pages show a snapshot of life in the area during the years of the Second World War.

Above right, in the event of enemy invasion a substantial wall built of round concrete blocks was constructed across the Market Place, South Cave, as seen here in this photograph. There were similar walls built across nearby Church Street and Beverley Road. In each case an opening was left to allow access for a single vehicle. In North Cave, a wall was built at the top of Westgate and another further down near the entrance to Blanshards Lane. Even in the small village of Hotham, a wall was built across Main Street. Alf Adamson remembers that at the height of the real threat of a German invasion there was a sentry posted on the road block situated outside his house, No. 22, Main Street for twenty four hours a day. To gain access a password had to be given. Much to the relief of the population of Great Britain the immediate threat of invasion had subsided by the end of 1940. Not only were the German airforce, the Lutwaffe, unable to gain air superiority over the Royal Air Force but the German Navy, known as the Kreigsmarine, found it impossible to supply sufficient invasion craft and surface warships with which to attempt the crossing of the English Channel.

In May 1940 Anthony Eden, Secretary of State for War, called for the formation of the Local Defence Volunteers (L. D. V.) Later they became known as the Home Guard. Volunteers throughout the land gave up their evenings and weekends for training in case of a German invasion. Members of the South Cave Home Guard are seen here on parade outside Cave Castle. Their headquarters were situated in an old wooden hut at the rear of the Bear Inn public house in the Market Place.

A formal photograph taken of the South Cave Home Guard outside the sandbagged Town Hall. These men and some three million like them nationwide were regarded as the visible public face of civilian defence against Hitler.

Frank Barratt who joined the South Cave Home Guard in 1940 recalls that surviving officers and sergeants from the First World War trained the men. Shortly after formation they were issued with uniforms, and rifles which could fire up to 900 yards and were extremely accurate. One of the best kept secrets of the war was that within many platoons nationwide a separate 'secret army' existed. It was Churchill's idea to recruit only the young and fit to form local guerilla resistance movements which would create havoc in the event of an invasion. While they trained in Home Guard uniform they had secret operations bunkers hidden usually in dense woodland which were full of the latest weapons and explosives. Frank Barratt was quietly approached in 1942 by his sergeant with the request that he should enlist with this 'secret army.' He declined as he was just about to be called up to serve in the regular army. It is known that a local gamekeeper accidently discovered the whereabouts of one of the bunkers in the area and revealed to one of the men guarding it that he knew exactly what it contained. It is said that, had there been an invasion the gamekeeper would have been executed to eliminate the risk of his revealing the whereabouts of the bunker to enemy invaders. It was deemed imperative that members of the 'secret army' should not be captured and thus secrecy was of the utmost importance.

Hotham and North Cave Home Guard in 1943. This photograph was taken outside their then headquarters at the old Boys' School, Westgate, North Cave.

Left, this Christmas party held in the Church Institute was organised as a final gathering before the South Cave Home Guard was disbanded in December 1944. Doug May a former member recalls there was plenty of beer, sandwiches and musical entertainment provided by a singer and pianist.

Below, a Hotham and North Cave Home Guard gathering in the Temperance Hall, Church Street, North Cave. This hall had become their headquarters in the latter part of the war.

Above right, some of the 17 'Bottle Bombs' (of the Molotov Cocktail type), which were unearthed in June 1964 in the grounds of the Bear Inn public house, South Cave together with a warning notice which was found with them. Mr. William Outhwaite, the licensee said, "We had just dismantled a shed and were levelling off the ground when the mechanical scoop picked up the bombs and exposed them." Ian Gibson and his brother John were the contractors on site and employed to prepare the area for a car park. Ian noticed that the bottles were full of yellow liquid and thought that they contained nothing more sinister than lemonade which had been discarded from the pub. He threw one against a wall and much to his shock and amazement the bottle exploded violently with a flash of fire. Army explosives experts soon arrived at the scene and the area was cordoned off until the bombs were disposed of. The old wooden hut which the Gibson brothers had just demolished had in fact been the headquarters of the South Cave Home Guard during the last war. The bombs had been buried yards from the hut under a pear tree in case of possible enemy invasion. Very near the Bear Inn were three road blocks and if there had been an enemy attack these bombs would have been used to throw at the invaders and their vehicles.

Another voluntary group, the Air Raid Precautions, (A.R.P.) was set up in 1939. Walter Brumfield, the chemist was head of the South Cave A.R.P. wardens whose duty it was to enforce the blackout regulations and if necessary survey and report any bomb damage to the control centre so that they could send the appropriate rescue services. From left to right, back row, n/k, Dr. Thompson, Billy Levick. Front row, Tom Moverley (motorcycle dispatch-rider), Harold Barrett, Fred Moore (bandmaster), Walter Brumfield (chemist), Alf Davies and George Hall (Headmaster of the Boys' School). The North Cave A.R.P. post was initially based in an old chicken hut in the Albion public house yard, and later a house in Church Street was used as their headquarters. Hotham's A.R.P. hut formerly stood on the site of the bus shelter next to the telephone box in Main Street. The hut door was left open at all times in case the phone rang. Alf Adamson a former member of the Hotham A.R.P. remembers the night of Saturday, 22nd February 1941, at five minutes to eight when two landmines dropped nearby. One did not detonate but the other exploded some 70 yards east of Hotham Hall, creating a crater 58 feet wide. Alf was at home playing the piano and having a sing-song with some of his neighbours when suddenly they heard a great explosion which seemed to cause the fireplace and range to shake out of the wall and go back again. On Monday, 5th May in the same year just after midnight two more landmines were dropped in the district. One landed at North Cave at the rear of All Saints' Church, causing some damage and the other struck at nearby Everthorpe, in a garden to the rear of number 4, High Road. There was one serious casualty, Mrs. Nan Waudby who was rushed to hospital where she recovered from her injuries and shock. There were several other minor casualties, with almost every house in the hamlet suffering at least some damage. Air Raid Warden Mrs. Florence Coates' home was so badly damaged that she and her family were evacuated to North Cave.

This photograph taken in 1941 outside No. 24, West End, shows members of the South Cave Auxiliary Fire Service with a hand pump which formed a main part of their equipment. It was carried about on Percy Gillatt's builders trailer and pulled by his car. Voluntary brigades such as this were trained for firefighting and anti-gas work. The local brigade would have been in attendance at a number of bombing incidents in the area during the Second World War. In one incident a serious fire occurred among parked

railway goods wagons after midnight on Wednesday, 10th March 1943 after a number of incendiary bombs had been dropped on North Cave railway station. Fortunately, there were no casualties. From left to right, Edgar Sims, Tom Ward with his dog, Ken Davies, Ernie Young, Mr. Ream and Percy Gillatt.

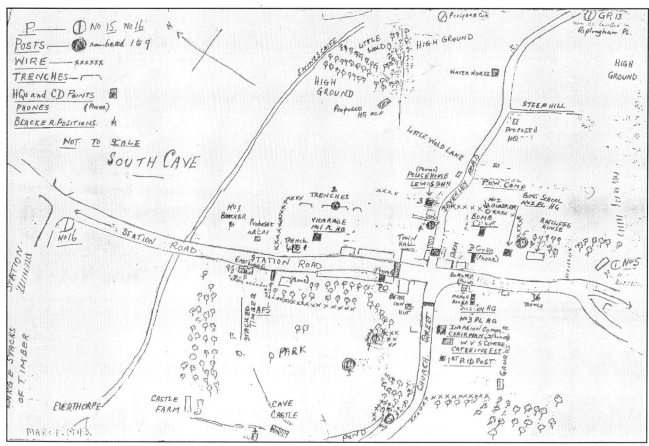

In the early years of the Second World War the threat of a surprise German invasion was all too real and many towns and villages such as South Cave had their own battle plans drawn up by the Home Guard in readiness. Above is a map showing the vital barricade positions and the buildings needed to effectively seal off the centre of the village from enemy attack.

Below, the opening ceremony of the South Cave 'Wings For Victory Week' which took place on Saturday, 29th May 1943. Standing in front of the fund raising indicator is the Committee, including Mr. J. W. Carmichael, who officially opened the event, Mr. J. W. Hickson (Chairman), and Mr. and Mrs. Walter Brumfield. The British public were strongly encouraged to save in order to keep inflation down and this as well as previous campaign efforts such as 'War Weapons' in 1941 and 'Warships' in 1942, had the added advantage of keeping up morale. In nearby Hotham, a village of only 260 inhabitants the 'Wings for Victory' campaign raised the astonishing total of £7,137. 17s 1d.

Right, members of the North Cave Women's Institute in fancy dress. The theme was "Dream of Empire." The W.I. was formed in 1927 and had its own choir which held concerts during the war in order to raise money to buy materials so that its members could make articles for the war effort. Working parties were formed to help with the many tasks including the evacuation of children and knitting garments for forces personnel.

War Weapons Week was an appeal to save money by buying either National War Bonds, Savings Certificates or simply by putting cash into deposit accounts at Post Office Savings Banks. The inhabitants of North Cave participated in this particular campaign during the first week of September 1941. Left, this group of officials and buyers of certificates are shown at the opening ceremony of the buying centre. During the week local schoolchildren together with evacuee children were visited by the Lord Mayor and Lady Mayoress of Kingston upon Hull. Concerts, dances, cinema shows, whist drives and sports events were arranged in order to raise money for this particular savings campaign. A total of £4,900 was raised exceeding the £4,000 target set for the village.

The Lord Mayor's (Councillor Sydney H. Smith), Air Raid Distress Fund came into being in February 1941. Donations flooded in following a wireless broadcast by the Lord Mayor in which he made a stirring appeal to the people of Hull and the surrounding districts to help the victims of bomb damage. Above, children from South Cave contributing by selling fresh fruit and vegetables from a stall to help raise money for the fund.

Left, members of the South Cave W.V.S. Soldiers billeted in the village used the canteen run by the Women's Voluntary Service which was situated in the Church Institute, in Church Street.

Following V. E. Day (Victory over Europe), on Tuesday, 8th May 1945, children's street parties celebrating the end of the war were held all over the country. Here is a children's Peace Party underway in Market Place, South Cave.

Left, this photograph taken sometime in the late 1950s shows members of the British Legion on Remembrance Sunday at the North Cave War Memorial. From the right stands Gordon Cooper, Billy Bond, n/k, n/k, Mrs. Bond (Standard Bearer for the Women's Section) and Mrs. Florence Coates.

Prisoners of War

Otto Wegener in the Prisoner Of War Camp situated at the rear of Cave Castle in 1944. Here Otto is seen in his Nissen hut (which he shared with 29 other prisoners), wearing civilian clothes. These were made by the camp tailor from old army blankets. The official uniform was a jacket with a large square on the back and a large circle on one of the trouser knees. It was only worn for working outside the camp and when the military police came to visit. The POWs were usually given advance notice of such visits! Inset, Otto as a young conscripted soldier in the German army.

Throughout the Second World War a number of regiments were based in the area. The 16th Field Regiment of the Royal Artillery was the first to move into Cave Castle in 1940, using it as their Headquarters. The owners Mr. Jimmy Carmichael and his family moved into the west lodge while officers from the regiment occupied the castle. The other ranks lived in huts within the castle grounds. One former soldier from the regiment, Fred Gratton, originally from Devon was billeted in one of the sheds within the stable yard. He was one of a number of soldiers who met their wives in the locality and decided to stay on after the war had ended.

Behind the stable yard there were a number of Nissen huts which housed German Prisoners Of War. These tunnel-shaped huts were made of corrugated iron and had a concrete floor. There were two other camps in the area which also held a number of German prisoners.

The camp at North Cave was situated adjacent to the old railway embankment where the present Fairfield estate now stands. The other camp which was erected in 1943 housed both Italian and German POWs and was situated at South Cave on an acre of land to the rear of Market Place Farm. The majority of POWs at this camp had been captured from Egypt after having been defeated at the Battle of El Alamein.

Land had been requisitioned from farmers nationally by the War Office in order to house the POWs and to provide extra labour because so many British men were fighting in the war. Following the end of the war the Market Place barracks were turned into quarters for pigs and chickens and then finally the huts were demolished.

In early 1993, a capping stone was discovered by a working party from H.M. Prison, Everthorpe which had been helping to clear rubbish from the beck near the old entrance to the Market Place camp. The stone was at one time positioned above the entrance to the camp and its inscription appears to read "POW CN73A XXIVVEF." However, its full meaning is not known. The stone was later incorporated into the side of a small bridge over the beck which leads to the entrance of a property on Beverley Road.

Many men spent a large portion of the Second World War experiencing life as POWs in these local camps. The majority of them had been conscripted into the forces and were relieved to have been captured by the British or Allied forces. Some were only too willing to work in the fields or in factories and a number of farmers and employers of these men report that they were hard workers and in some cases struck up friendly

The POW inscription which is now incorporated into a small bridge over the beck on Beverley Road, South Cave.

relationships with them. The following stories are characteristic of two typical conscripts who, like other men in their position, decided to stay in Britain after the war ended.

Otto Wegener

Otto Wegener, was born in 1922 in eastern Germany in Boecka, a small village near Berlin. He was 17 years old and an apprentice painter and decorator when he received papers to report to the German army.

On arrival he was sent by train to a labour camp in Konitc, Poland. Along with other boys he worked in a brickyard loading red hot bricks straight from the kiln into waiting trucks. He had no idea why he was there until an officer later informed him that it was because he had declined an earlier invitation to join the Hitler Youth Movement.

After six months he was released but within days had received call up papers again to report to the German army, in which he was conscripted into the 'A' Company Infantry Division as an ordinary soldier. After six months basic training he was sent to fight at the Russian front. Later, his Company was sent to the Ukraine where Otto was badly wounded and was transferred to hospital.

He underwent an operation and was then sent with other soldiers who were classed as 90% fit to occupy Norway. In 1944 following a few months of appalling weather conditions in that country, Otto's regiment was taken by ship back to northern Germany where they made a long journey travelling thirty men per cattle truck to Le Havre in Normandy, France.

On the morning of Tuesday, 6th June 1944 from the brow of a hill they watched through binoculars as the biggest land, sea and air operation of all time began. This great invasion is remembered today as D-Day.

The Allied forces consisting of 75,000 British and Canadian

troops together with 57,000 American troops were involved in the operation. In the sky there were 13,000 aircraft, 27,000 airborne troops and 867 gliders. Having crossed the English Channel they landed on the beaches of Normandy gaining the strategic foothold that would lead to the liberation of Western Europe from the German occupiers.

Within days Otto's regiment was captured by the rapidly approaching Americans. They were now prisoners of war and were escorted to a large holding compound on the beach. Each soldier was issued with a numbered tag which identified the country to which he would be transported as a POW.

Otto, unhappy at the thought of going to far away America swapped his identity number with another POW who had a British number tag. Shortly afterwards, POWs bound for England were escorted on foot to Dieppe to another holding camp. Finally, they boarded an empty tank landing ship with hundreds of other German POWs bound for Southampton.

On arrival, they were taken by train to Kempton Park Race Course, near London which had been turned into a huge transit camp for enemy aliens. Members of the Salvation Army gave the newly arrived POWs as much soup, bread, coffee and tea as they wanted.

Following registration and a three hour interrogation session Otto was issued with his identity papers and sent north by train with other low risk POWs, where he spent time in Storwood Camp, then Bretton Camp near Selby, before finally arriving at POW Camp 53 on Station Road, North Cave.

Otto recalls that there were about sixty POWs at this camp and every Sunday about half of them would walk from the camp to All Saints' Church in the village where they would be greeted with a hymn book and bible. Very few of them understood the English language but recognised the words 'God' and 'Jesus' and took part in the service as well as they could, visually following the actions of the regular congregation.

Those who were skilled tradesmen, such as Otto and who volunteered to work were assigned to the industrial sector and those without skills were given employment in the agricultural sector. Otto and other prisoners were collected each day by army truck and taken to work at a sugar factory in York. They were given a shilling a day which was generally regarded as being worthless as it could only be spent in the camp on general articles such as toiletries.

In order to compensate for this, sugar, jars of jam and sweets were smuggled out of the factory in small quantities and sold to local people through an intermediary. English money was saved and at regular intervals a German professor POW who could speak fluent English and who worked with them at the factory, would be given a shopping list for purchases which he would make when browsing around the shops in York!

He would come back laden with the materials ordered by his fellow POWs which they would use back at the camp to produce items such as toys, leather goods, guitars and small general household items made from wood. Hessian sacks which had contained sugar were also acquired from the factory and transformed into slippers. All these items were sold through their intermediary outlet.

Otto was later transferred to the POW camp at the back of the stable yard at Cave Castle, South Cave but still continued to work for the sugar factory. He recalls that at both camps there was very little security with usually only five strands of barbed wire around the perimeter of each camp and prisoners were unofficially allowed to stroll around the village provided they behaved themselves and did not go into shops

Otto shortly before his retirement at the age of 75 years in May 1998. In 1981 Otto, who retired from his job after 22 years as an inspector at a local engineering firm, became increasingly concerned at the amount of litter in the Main Street of Market Weighton. At his own expense he purchased bin bags, a brush and wheelbarrow and began to regularly sweep the Main Street. Following five years of voluntary work, the town council declared him to be an official street cleaner and paid him a nominal wage. On several occasions he was awarded certificates for his work, including second place in a national competition for "Street Cleaner of The Year".

or openly fraternize with the local inhabitants.

Otto finally left the South Cave camp after nine months and spent the rest of the war in a number of other camps in the north of England, including Hut 10 at Eden Camp, Malton, North Yorkshire (now opened as a museum). In October 1949 all POW camps in Britain finally closed and Otto was sent from Melbourne Camp near Market Weighton, where he had been working for East Riding Transport, back to Germany.

Shortly following his arrival at the huge transit camp in Munster Lager, West Germany, Otto, along with other compatriots who had originated from eastern Germany were informed that if they returned to their homes which were then under the control of the Russians, they would be regarded as enemy spies and could expect to serve at least five years in a labour camp. As a result very few of them decided to return to the east and many like Otto returned to England to live. In fact, Otto returned to his former job for a time with East Riding Transport and lived in a caravan in Holme Road, Market Weighton. He later met and married Winnie, a local girl and they made their home in the district.

Jorg (George) Aniol and his wife Kitty.

Jorg (George) Aniol

Jorg (George), Aniol was another former German POW who settled in the area after the war. His involvement in the Second World War began in 1939 when at the age of 17 years he was drafted into the Kreismarine, the German Navy. Following a short training course he was given the position of a U-boat submariner.

For the next four and a half years Jorg served on a succession of U-boats and on one patrol in the North Sea, he was actually to see the East Yorkshire coastline for the first time through a periscope from about three miles off Bridlington. Afterwards he told how he could clearly distinguish the white mass of the 'Expanse Hotel' on Bridlington's north shore.

On the way down to the English Channel on the 6th June 1944 (D-Day) and in an attempt to interrupt the Allied landings in Normandy, Jorg's vessel, travelling on the surface, was bombed and sunk by an RAF Mosquito.

Jorg had been on deck with eleven other men at the time. When the U-boat blew up Jorg was hurled into the sea and was subsequently picked up by a Royal Navy destroyer. From a crew of eighty men there were only five other survivors. When the destroyer docked at Southampton, Jorg and his fellow survivors were taken under escort to a prisoner of war camp nearby.

He was subsequently transferred to a POW camp situated at the rear of Cave Castle, South Cave and later moved on to the North Cave POW camp which was next to the railway embankment where the present Fairfield estate stands. Jorg was given work on various farms in the district.

When the camps eventually closed after the war, Jorg opted not to return to eastern Germany but to stay in North Cave. Jorg became known as 'George' and was well liked and respected in the village. He eventually married Kitty Chapman a local girl and worked for thirty years for Capper Pass Limited at Melton, North Ferriby. Owing to a chronic spine condition he was forced to take early retirement. George who lived in Church Street, North Cave died at the age of 73 years in February 1995.

Les Williamson

Life as a prisoner of war, however, was not so comfortable for local man Les Williamson. Les was born in South Cave and at the age of twenty he was called up to join the East Yorkshire Regiment in 1940, when after basic training he was placed in the 4th Battalion.

While serving in North Africa, Les, together with hundreds of other soldiers from his Battalion and the Green Howards which combined were known as the 150th Brigade, were captured by Field Marshall, Erwin Rommel and his troops, during the first day of the battle of Ghazala on the 2nd June 1942.

Rommel's clever tactics had earned him the nickname "The Desert Fox." Marching past the Field Marshall's bell-tent, only a matter of ten yards away, Les saw Rommel standing in the doorway closely observing the captured British soldiers. Now a POW, he joined the rest of his Battalion who were being loaded into Fiat trucks. They were taken by armed guard to Derhana, on the coast road where they spent a week in a walled graveyard which had been adapted to serve as a makeshift POW camp.

The captured troops were then taken further along the coast road to Tripoli where they were placed in a compound containing about 1,000 men with little food and no proper medical or sanitary facilities. Every day a new large ditch which served as the camp latrine was dug and the old one filled in. As a result of these conditions dysentery, typhus and lice were soon rife in the compound

Three weeks later all the POWs were transferred to the hold of a cargo ship, where they were locked in until the ship arrived at Taranto, southern Italy. On arrival they were allowed a shower, their clothes were fumigated and everyone had their heads shaved and dipped in a bucket of paraffin to kill the lice.

Later, they were sent to Carpi, a little village in Northern Italy to POW camp PG 73 which consisted of two large compounds containing altogether about 4,000 prisoners of different nationalities. Once in the camp they found that they were crammed into huts of up to 100 inmates.

For more than a year, Les, like everyone else there, endured a continual fight for survival. Only one meal a day was served which was known as 'skilly' a thin watery vegetable soup. As well as the constant problem of lice Les recalls, *"Once you got over the sight of men starving or writhing in agony, it was a battle not to lose your mind. We walked miles everyday around the perimeter just to keep going."* Occasional Red Cross parcels which often had to be shared between two or three men, provided their only luxuries. These usually contained items such as cigarettes, coffee, tea, concentrated biscuits, jam, skimmed milk, sugar, corned beef, chocolate and soap.

In July 1943 news reached the camp that Sicily had been invaded and that Italy was surrendering. Les and his fellow prisoners all believed they would soon be free but it was a false dawn. Early next morning and armed with machine guns the Germans surrounded the camp and a section totalling about 900 British prisoners, including Les, were loaded into cattle trucks destined for POW camp Stalag 8B in Germany.

After travelling through the Brenner Pass in Italy, the train ground to a halt and all POWs were told to disembark and form a long column for inspection. Les remembers seeing a group of about 15 boys and a number of young men from the Hitler Youth Movement, walking slowly up and down the line looking at them face to face. The youths were told that these captured men were part of the enemy they would have to face one day when their turn came to join the German Army.

Eventually, following a short spell in Stalag 8B Camp, Les was

Taken at Carpi POW camp by a German propaganda photographer, Les Williamson (left) and fellow soldier and friend Glen Sutherby. Photographs were bartered for cigarettes and POWs were then encouraged to send the photographs home to reassure their families of their well-being, which was often very far from the truth. Fortunate to survive the harsh conditions as a POW, when Les, (a healthy 10 stone lorry driver before the war) was finally released he weighed just over seven stones.

transported to a labour camp at Yavosno, near Krakov, Poland, where for 14 months he was forced to work long shifts down a coal mine.

Every day armed guards would escort POWs to and from the mine some three miles away from the labour camp. The camp was in fact only ten miles away from the notorious concentration camp at Auschwitz. Les remembers that," *We used to see all the Jews going in the trucks and could smell the fires which always seemed to be burning. It was dreadful.*"

Food was scarce and their rations were barely enough for survival. The occasional Red Cross parcels were heavily relied upon to supplement the prisoners' diet. The biscuits contained in the parcels would be pooled and ground into flour with which the camp cook would make a sort of milk pudding. Items such as chocolate could be exchanged under a bartering system with the local Poles who also worked in the mine, for boiled eggs.

One morning all the POWs were woken and told to get their kit together. Forming a column, they picked up more POWs as they went along, until there were about 1,000 men. None of the POWs could have known then that they would still be marching some four months and 1,000 miles later.

Each night they would stop at a farm and following a meal of watery soup they would be split up into smaller groups and locked in barns until the next morning. Les recalls that," *One night we heard shots. Next morning two lads were lying dead outside one of the barns. We were told that would be our fate too if anyone else tried to escape.*"

That did not prevent a further breakout being attempted a few weeks later. Disgusted with the appalling food and conditions a small group of men decided one morning to hide and wait until the column had moved off before making their escape.

A few hours later they came across an isolated farm where they requested some food. The farmer invited them in but while they were eating he telephoned the German Military Police who came and picked them up and returned them to the column. Fortunately, their only punishment was to be segregated every night and locked securely into a hen hut.

In April 1945 and 1,000 miles later the POW column had reached Bavaria. One evening the German officer in charge revealed to the senior British officer that the Americans would probably be arriving in a matter of hours.

Early next morning the German officer had disappeared and with only two guards left in charge they awaited the arrival of the Americans. Later, a jeep drew up and American soldiers asked if they were British. When satisfied that they were they opened the gates to let them out and took away the two remaining German guards. Les remembers that some of the lads went off on bicycles, even though there was sniper fire. The rest of the men stayed in the compound wondering what to do next.

After a while Les and his compatriots realised they would have to fend for themselves. A former butcher in the ranks shot a bullock and it was roasted over a fire. Some of the men went into the local village and brought back pigs, chickens and ducks for the men to eat.

It was not until about two weeks later that trucks were finally sent to pick them up. They were all taken to an airport about 40 miles away and boarded air ambulances destined for a British army camp in Brussels. On arrival, Les recalls they were each given a white handkerchief and a bar of chocolate. After two days they were finally on their way home to England.

In May 1945 Les finally arrived home in South Cave to a joyful reunion with his father William but was devastated to learn that his mother Caroline had died unexpectedly just two months earlier. He was demobbed later that year and returned to lorry driving for a living. He married in 1952 and today lives in well earned retirement in South Cave with his wife

Les Williamson in 1998.

Everthorpe

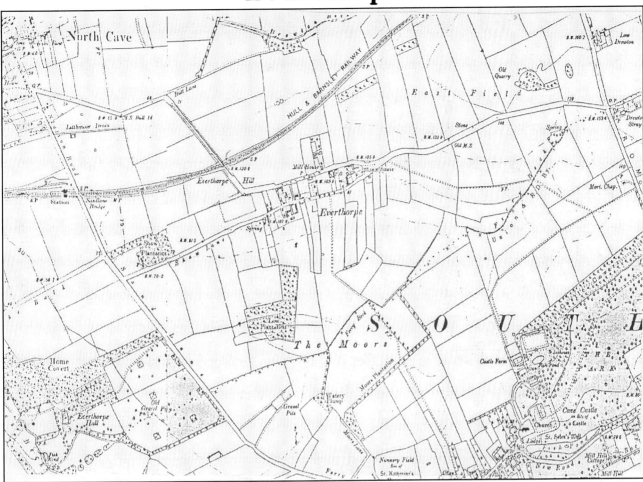

Map of Everthorpe 1910

Everthorpe is a hamlet situated between North Cave and South Cave. A number of interesting artefacts have been discovered in the area which include a hoard of 16 Bronze Age axes. The hoard was found in 1842 at the site of a gravel pit alongside the old Hull and Barnsley West Junction Railway where the High Road bridge crosses it in Everthorpe. The axes were unusually wedge-shaped and were found with two large ingots of bronze apparently taken from a crucible.

In 1929 a Bronze Age burial site was unearthed during excavations in a nearby sandpit. Evidence of burials from later periods show that there have been other succeeding settlements in the area. For example, during the construction of the Hull and Barnsley West Junction Railway, (1882-84), a number of skeletons wearing Roman helmets were found at the Everthorpe cutting. Other discoveries found in 1958 in the vicinity of Everthorpe Hall suggest that a site then being prepared for a prison recreation ground was formerly an Anglian inhumation cemetery dating to around the 4-5th century A.D.

It is clear therefore, that the area has been settled from prehistoric times but we have to move to 1083 to the time of the Domesday Survey to get the first documented details of settlement in Everthorpe. During the compilation of the Domesday Book which was completed in 1086 a great many hamlets and villages including Everthorpe had been omitted but were included in a summary at the end of the book.

No explanation exists as to why they were not included in the main survey, but most of these places, including Everthorpe were amongst the possessions of Count Robert Mortain. Count Mortain, according to the famous Bayeux tapestry rode at the side of William the Conqueror (his half brother), at the battle of Hastings in 1066.

At the time of the survey Everthorpe is shown as having, *"Five carucates of culture, with its fallow ..."* which was about 100 acres and it was tenanted by Count Mortain to a Nigel Fossard. It is mentioned again in 1128 as *Yvertorp* and in 1130 as *Ivertorp*.

No record is made of Everthorpe as having the status of a separate Manor until 1330, when it was passed by the method of a fine, registering the transaction from Thomas Saltmarshe to John Hay.

The Manor of Everthorpe subsequently descended to the Askes of Aughton. In 1593 a John Aske sold the Manor to Hugh Bethell. John was the brother of Robert Aske who had led the Pilgrimage of Grace in 1536. Robert was later executed for his part in the uprising but John remained loyal to King Henry VIII.

In 1593-4 Hugh Bethell of Ellerton, later Sir Hugh purchased Everthorpe Manor which remained in the Bethell family until 1803 when W. J. Bethell sold it to Joseph Egginton. Joseph was a Hull shipowner and one of his whaling ships built by Gleadow of Hull in 1810 was named the *"Everthorpe"*.

In 1828 the Manor was settled on Joseph's son, John Smyth Egginton. John and his wife Louisa had six children and it was their eldest son John Gostling Egginton who inherited the Everthorpe estate following his father's death in 1848.

John a captain in H.M. 41st Regiment, sold the estate to Joseph Gee in 1857. His nephew Thomas Stephen Whitaker inherited the estate following his death in 1860.

Everthorpe Hall

There are no records available to inform us as to where the original Manor House was situated although a Hall Garth is known to have existed in 1637 and Hall Crofts lay at the west end of the hamlet in 1774.

In 1870 Everthorpe Hall, situated about one mile south-west of the hamlet, was built for Thomas S. Whitaker on the site of an earlier property near Mires Beck, known as Everthorpe Cottage (built c.1811).

Following Thomas Whitaker's death in June 1912 the estate was divided and sold in 1913-14. The East Riding County Council bought the manor and about 500 acres in Everthorpe.

The Hall stood empty for some time until 1914 when it was purchased by Mr. Benjamin Shaw Seed of Hessle, a partner in John Seed & Sons, Fruit Brokers of Humber Street, Hull. His son John Humphrey Allison Seed inherited the property in 1928. He sold Everthorpe Hall and the 130 acre estate in 1947 to Gilbert Baitson a well known Hull auctioneer.

In June 1949 owing to a public outcry the proposals for converting Cave Castle as the site for a new security prison were abandoned. The Prison Commission then turned their attention to the possibility of acquiring Everthorpe Hall a mile to the north west of Cave Castle.

After much persuasion Mr. Baitson sold Everthorpe Hall to the Home Office and the prison authorities converted it at a cost of about £1,000,000 into a security training prison, which was initially opened as a borstal. At the time, this was the first new prison to be built in England since 1919.

Built by F. Shepherd and Son Ltd., of York the prison consisted of two main cell blocks of 3 storeys each, and containing 154 cells. There was also a large administration block and other ancillary buildings.

The foundation stone was laid by the Home Secretary, Major Gwilym Lloyd George on Saturday, 21st April 1956. A considerable area of the parkland was enclosed behind an 18 ft. high precast and prestressed concrete wall as a security measure and about 55 houses were built to accommodate the Governor, prison officers and ancillary staff.

In 1989 work began building the first privately-operated British prison. Completed in 1991 The Wolds Remand Prison was built adjacent to H.M. Prison Everthorpe. Three indentical two-storey house-blocks constructed of reinforced concrete clad in yellow brick accommodate 100 inmates per house. Other blocks include an entry gatehouse, kitchen, reception, segregation and medical areas as well as a chapel, gymnasium and library.

Everthorpe Hall (West Front), is a castellated two-storey house of yellow brick, with projecting three-storey entrance tower. The Hall is now used as the staff club for Her Majesty's Prison, Everthorpe and is also the headquarters of the North Cave-South Cave British Legion.

A feature of the entrance to the prison which occupies the Everthorpe Hall grounds are the two stone lions which guard each side of the gateway on their ashlar plinths. They were originally installed by former owner Benjamin Shaw Seed in front of the Hall itself (see above), but were later resited by the prison authorities to the main entrance of the prison. Dating from c.1875 and made by W. D. Keyworth of London these carved limestone sculptures once flanked the drive of a house in Anlaby Road, Hull which is now occupied by East Yorkshire Motor Services Ltd.

In 1947 an achery club known as the 'Bowmen of Holderness' was formed. Gilbert Baitson was one of the club's leading members and during his occupancy of Everthorpe Hall he regularly invited members to use his grounds in which an area had been especially designated for target practice. Here on the right of this photograph Gilbert is seen with his long bow and other members of the archery club who are congregated around one of the old stone lions then situated in front of the Hall.

Gilbert Baitson was also a keen motor cycle racing enthusiast and organised races in the grounds as seen above. To the left, Gilbert is photographed standing in front of the Hall with banners displayed in the background requesting a 4d. entrance fee to one such event.

Everthorpe Village

The small estate hamlet lies to the east of Everthorpe Hall. Although there are a few stone-built farms here including Milestone Farm with the date 1784 shown on the side of the farmhouse, the settlement is predominately residential without any shopping facilities.

In the early-mid 19th century the hamlet was quite a thriving self supporting community with a population of 83 inhabitants. Situated on the High Road was a public house known as the Duke of York and also a windmill for grinding corn. Records reveal that the hamlet even appointed its own officers including a pinder, surveyor and constable.

The Duke of York public house closed about 1871 following the departure of William Holmes the landlord to North Cave where he opened a flesh and bone manure business.

Sometime during the early 1870s the Pearson family, who were the village joiners, blacksmiths, wheelwrights and builders, opened a general grocery store combined with a post office in premises annexed to the former inn. Later in c.1888 the post office moved to Cunnyworth Cottage further along the High Road. The post office closed during the Second World War.

When the estate was sold in 1913 the East Riding County Council purchased a total of eight farms and added them to their smallholding estate. Over the years a few of these farms consisting of approximately 50 acres each became uneconomical to continue. As a consequence the farmhouses were sold and the land added to other local farms which are still owned by the East Riding County Council.

Above, the former Duke of York, an 18th century public house is now a private residence known as No. 4, High Road. It was originally a long low stone building but has been extensively renovated over the years, especially in c.1923 when the Pearson family demolished the old adjoining post office and grocery store, erecting a cottage on either side of the building. Between c.1900-1925, Edward and Alice Langrick ran a grocery store from the above premises. Geoff Hardwick the present owner remembers that there was a huge Yorkshire range fireplace in one of the front downstairs rooms which was used by Alice who regularly baked bread for the residents of nearby Everthorpe Hall.

Left, taken earlier this century this photograph of the High Road shows Cunneyworth Cottage with ground floor shutters. For many years part of the property was used as the village post office. Further along on the right, is Mill Farm.

Right, a pleasant rural scene. This view was taken on the Low Road, Everthorpe around the turn of the century. Throughout the 20th century the hamlet has remained relatively unspoiled and undeveloped. .

Everthorpe Windmill in 1890. The flour mill once formed part of Mill Farm, on the High Road. The last miller was Alfred Houseman who was also a cattle dealer and farmer. Windmills had been in decline for some years by the time Alfred began farming here and it seems likely that he would have used the mill mainly for grinding corn for his cattle. During the 19th century there had been a general move from stone-grinding to the new metal roller-grinders. At the same time steam power was coming into use. Large flour-mills were erected at many ports including Hull, where cheaper foreign wheat was being imported. As a consequence country windmills and watermills were gradually made redundant. Everthorpe windmill was struck by lightning in 1895. Tragically, the remains of the mill collapsed during its demolition and killed the man engaged on this work. Members of the Houseman family are pictured here standing in front of the old windmill in 1890 with their baby grandson John William Cade.

Left, an old dovecote which was part of Cote Farm on Low Road, Everthorpe. It was demolished in September 1987 as it had fallen into serious disrepair; the south wall having almost entirely collapsed. Below, could this be the last remaining resident poignantly posing prior to the building's demolition?

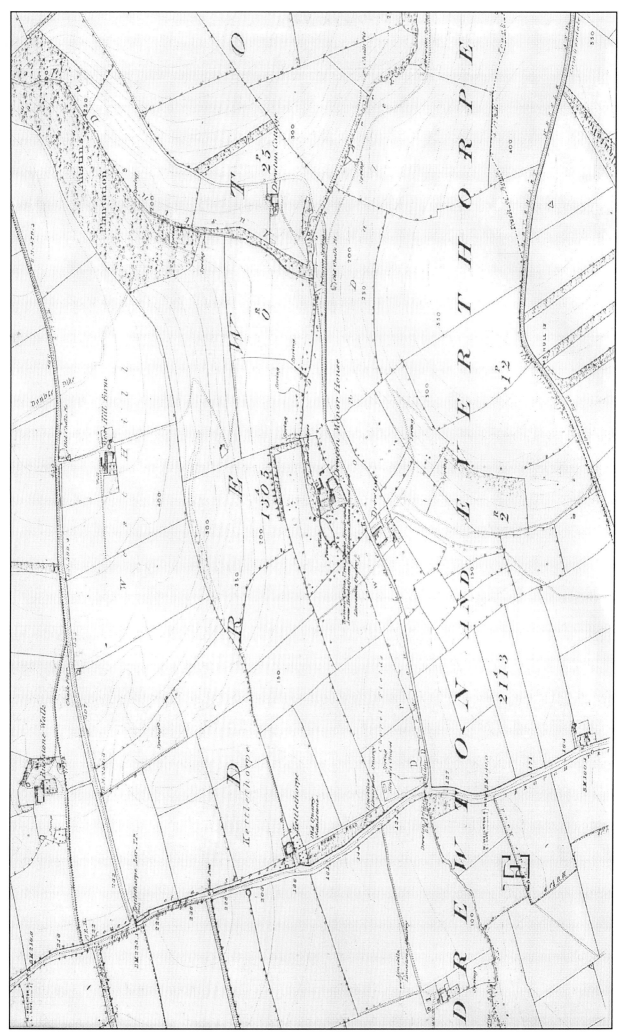

Map of Drewton 1850

Drewton

Drewton lies about one and a half miles north east of South Cave and about two miles east of North Cave. In the Domesday Book it was referred to under Drowetone (Drewton) as, *"In Torp (Thorp) Chetel (Ketel) had two carucates of land to be taxed and there may be one plough there. Robert Malet has it, and it is waste."*

It is known that a medieval hamlet named Kettlethorpe once existed near there. Kettlethorpe farmhouse, built c.1775, may well stand very near the former hamlet mentioned in the Domesday Book of 1086. A little further north of Kettlethorpe is Rudstone Walk Farm, which dates back 400 years. Its name was derived from the medieval hamlet of 'Rudtope' which once existed nearby.

Records show that Drewton contained a watermill in 1100 with a further two being recorded in 1540 and 1620. The settlement appears as a vill or feudal township in the Norman villarum of 1316. Later, in 1533 there were forced evictions by Sir Robert Constable, at the time when much land around the Wolds was allowed to change from arable to pasture in favour of sheep farming.

Nevertheless, the hamlet seems to have survived until at least the late 17th century, since a Chapel Close is mentioned in 1616 and a total of 13 houses was recorded in 1672. It is known that a chapel stood on the eastern side of the Market Weighton Road near Drewton Bridge. Until the late 19th century the foundations of the chapel and the remains of its graveyard could be still seen before they became completely overgrown.

Earlier that century, local Minister, the Reverend John Allen in his book, *'A Strangers Guide to Ferriby, Welton, Elloughton and South Cave,'* remarked that, *"A number of foundations had been found in the vicinity ... and all the stones found had the mark of fire upon them, as though the houses of which they had formed a part had been burned down."*

Unfortunately, no records survive to explain the reason why Drewton was burnt down. Perhaps the village had been turned over to sheep farming, or maybe it was the result of a skirmish. It still remains unclear.

By the late 18th century Drewton consisted of only Drewton Manor House and a farmhouse until four houses were built in the mid-20th century. A lane leading from the Market Weighton Road was diverted away from the Manor House in 1841.

Many ancient relics have been found in this area especially in the vicinity of Drewton Manor. These include a number of Roman artefacts and coins as well as human bones. During the mid-19th century several skeletons were discovered buried side by side, one of them decapitated.

Later during the early 1880s when the Hull, Barnsley and West Riding Junction Railway was being constructed several more skeletons were uncovered. It is believed by archeologists that the construction workers had stumbled upon a Roman execution site.

One of the most curious Roman finds was a lachrymatory, or small vessel, wherein the tears of the weeping family and friends of deceased persons were reposited and buried with the ashes and urns of the dead.

Drewton Manor situated near the junction of two steep sided valleys is thought to date from c.1774. The property built of local limestone was renovated in 1840 and again in c.1900. In 1844 Mr. George Baron (d.1854), inherited the manor house and about 500 acres of land in Drewton from his mother Sarah. Mr. Baron discovered a number of Roman artefacts in the vicinity of the property which included a silver ring in the form of a snake, brooches, spear heads, arrow heads and pottery. On acquiring some land near to his estate Mr. Baron, in an effort to improve its quality, required the channel of Drewton Beck to be lowered by 2 feet in order to provide some underdrainage. This revealed, at about 22 yards to the east of the bridge crossing the beck, a portion of the Roman Road from Brough (Petuaria). Mr. Baron personally traced the road about 70 yards northwards at a depth of 4 feet below the surface. In later years it was traced to the garden of Kettlethorpe farmhouse. Drewton Manor was later occupied by Alderman Charles Richardson, J.P. who was Lord Mayor of Kingston upon Hull for three successive years (1893-95). He died at Drewton Manor aged 54 years on the 8th June 1898. Following a succession of owners Drewton Manor and the estate were sold to Mr. Graham Hellyer in 1977 who still possessed them in 1999.

Saint Augustine's Stone

Saint Augustine's or Saint Austin's stone stands in Drewton Dale about half a mile to the north-east of Drewton.

It is a mass of rock measuring some sixty feet long, twenty feet wide and ten feet high, projecting from the side of a hill and being split into two principal masses.

The stone is believed to have received its name from the visit of Saint Augustine to the East Riding, although through the centuries the name appears to have been shortened to Saint Austin.

During the 6th century Saint Augustine and forty other monks were sent to Anglia (England), by Pope Gregory I, to convert the natives to Christianity. Pope Gregory had witnessed four fair haired children being sold as slaves in Rome. He compared them to angels and on making enquiries was informed they had come from the Kingdom of Deira (East Riding of Yorkshire).

Saint Augustine arrived in Kent in 597 A.D. and converted Ethelbert, King of Kent and many of his followers. During his missionary activities Saint Augustine is reputed to have visited Drewton in the Kingdom of Deira and preached Christianity to the local Saxons from the stone.

Although the story of such a visit has been passed down through the centuries in local folklore there is no written account to support this tradition. Moreover, historians believe it is extremely doubtful that he ever came as far north as Drewton. Certainly, paganism flourished in the kingdom long after the death of Saint Augustine.

This mysterious pile of stone is believed to have been used formerly as a site of Druidical worship and that the actual name of Drewton (or Druid Town), is derived from Celtic times when Druidism was the religion of the Celtic people of the pre-Christian British Isles and Gaul (France).

It is thought that the Druids may have used the stone as an altar in their religious worship. Wise in the lore of plants, animals and stars, they were also magicians and astrologers. The oak tree was sacred to the Druids and their rites were often practiced in an oak forest. It is known that up until the 18th century there was an abundance of oak trees on and around the site of the stone.

Their religion which simply believed in the immortality of the human soul and the existence of one supreme being, was unfortunately marred by human and animal sacrifices. It is not known however, if any such sacrifices were ever made at this particular site.

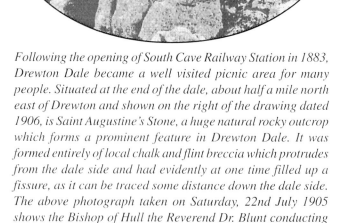

Following the opening of South Cave Railway Station in 1883, Drewton Dale became a well visited picnic area for many people. Situated at the end of the dale, about half a mile north east of Drewton and shown on the right of the drawing dated 1906, is Saint Augustine's Stone, a huge natural rocky outcrop which forms a prominent feature in Drewton Dale. It was formed entirely of local chalk and flint breccia which protrudes from the dale side and had evidently at one time filled up a fissure, as it can be traced some distance down the dale side. The above photograph taken on Saturday, 22nd July 1905 shows the Bishop of Hull the Reverend Dr. Blunt conducting an open air service at the stone to a congregation consisting largely of local Sunday School teachers. The stone is now fenced off and stands on private property.

This pilgrim badge found at Drewton by Stephen Foster shows St. Thomas Becket of Canterbury and dates to about the end of the 14th century. Made of lead, it is one of the many popular types of souvenirs that pilgrims would collect travelling around religious sites. It seems quite likely that the stone was one such site they visited thus carrying on the local tradition that Saint Augustine, appointed the first Archbishop of Canterbury in 601 A.D. once preached there.

The Hunsley Beacons

A Beacon is a primitive system of communication over long distances. It has been used since prehistoric times as an early warning alarm of attack. The earliest record of a beacon at High Hunsley is in 1536 during the period of the Dissolution of the Monasteries under King Henry VIII when thousands of inhabitants from the East Riding met there under the banner of the "Pilgrimage of Grace".

This Yorkshire rebellion had one common cause which cut across all social boundaries. That was to restore the Roman Catholic Church and reopen the monasteries. In 1536 with 40,000 men from all over Yorkshire, their leader Robert Aske set out to march to London, but disbanded on the promise that a Parliament would be held in York. However, when this did not happen further outbreaks of violence occurred. Aske was subsequently arrested and taken in chains to York, where, with other rebels he was hanged. As a consequence the revolt collapsed.

Later in the century and following the threat of a Spanish invasion in 1586, a chain of beacons was erected all along the coasts of England to warn of any approach by the Spanish Armada. Hunsley had, " ... *two beacons takinge lighte from Bainton, and geveth lighte to Holme"*. This beacon of Hunsley, like those of Holme on the Wolds and Bainton, gives its name to a Division of the Riding.

Three centuries after any threat of invasion had passed one of the Hunsley beacons still survived until around the early 19th century. It stood at the highest point of the road from Drewton to High Hunsley, in the corner of an arable field.

At the top of the pole was a shallow tub, which was supported by three tall props reaching nearly to the top. The steps to reach the barrel were cross pieces of wood on one of the supports.

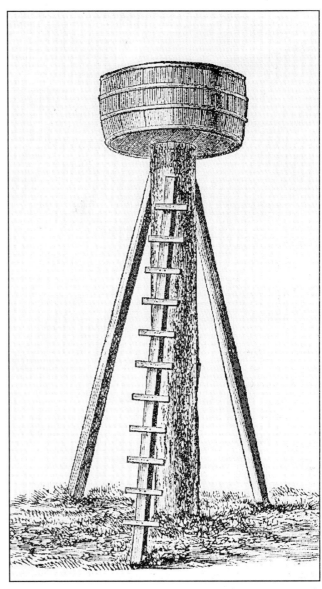

Above, a sketch of one of the surviving Hunsley Beacons made c.1830, from a description by Mr. J. Boodie, of Hull. A shallow wooden tub has replaced the usual iron cage at the top of the pole and it appears that the use of the beacon had changed to that of a lookout post.

Double Dikes

Dikes such as those found in the Drewton area are frequently found in the Yorkshire Wolds from Bridlington to the River Humber. Of these, the Danes Dykes are probably the most important. Some are single, others double and some triple earthworks.

The commonly held view of historians is that the dikes were constructed by ancient peoples inhabiting the high ground, as defensive works. In this area, invaders advancing from either the Vale of York or the Holderness plains east of Hull could be seen.

These dikes are invariably associated with cairn groups, urn-barrows or similar constructions and are believed to date from the Middle Bronze Age. All the more noticeable works stand across ancient ridgeways defined by round barrows.

In general, the bank is formed merely by the earth thrown out of the ditch, but quite often it is surmounted by a parapet of upright stones. Some of the lines are of considerable length, but usually they obstruct narrow passes or cross projecting hills.

The dikes occur almost invariably on the steeper slopes of the Yorkshire Wolds and so have a most commanding position. It is thought quite likely that the dikes themselves which vary in depth to as much as seven or eight feet, were used as a means of ensuring a safe passage from one point to another during the threat of attack by enemies.

This photograph was taken on Wednesday, 4th June 1932 and shows a group from The Workers Educational Association led by South Cave historian Archie Trout exploring ancient earthworks in the area.

Transport

It is difficult to imagine that for centuries travelling any long distance for the majority of the population was very rare; pack-horses and mules carried the lighter wares of merchants, while their heavier goods went by river craft.

About the middle of the seventeenth century the stage coach was introduced, becoming a regular means of travel after 1660. These heavy vehicles caused deep ruts in the roads which in the main were no more than trackways and maintenance was generally poor.

The improvement of the roads was left almost entirely to groups of individuals who formed themselves into Turnpike Trusts, taking over sections of roads after obtaining consent by means of a private Act of Parliament. Between 1760 and 1820 over 1,000 of these Acts were passed.

The road from Brough to Newbald was turnpiked in 1771 coming under the Brough Ferry - South Newbald Holmes Turnpike Trust and ran for a distance of 8.2 miles. The Trust consisted mainly of local merchants, landowners and farmers who in 1771 had an Act passed by Parliament,

"For repairing and widening the road from the Low Water Mark of the River Humber, at or near Brough Ferry, in the parish of Elloughton, in the East Riding of the County of York, to the North End of the town of Brough, and thence through South Cave to Coney Clappers in South Newbald Holmes in the said Riding."

A toll house was erected at the junction of Cave Road and Welton Road in Brough and another was built at Kettlethorpe, on the north eastern road from South Cave. Toll bars were also placed across the road outside the houses and would only be lifted by the toll house keeper when he had received payment by those wishing to use the road. The collected tolls were used by the local Turnpike Trust for the general maintenance of the road.

There was however, another turnpike road which ran through Swinescaife Road in the parish of South Cave and which was part of the Howden to Hull route. Under an Act of 1774 the Beverley and Hessle Turnpike Trust extended their interest to the road leading from Kirkella churchyard past Raywell and Riplingham to North Cave and thence to, " ... *a drain or canal on a common called Wallingfen, leading to Howden."*

Tolls were charged according to the type of vehicle and number of animals passing through the gate. The charge for carriages drawn by one horse, ox or ass, was initially set at 1d. to pass through the turnpike gates. A sum of half a penny was charged for animals laden or unladen not drawing a wheeled vehicle, and drovers of oxen or cattle paid the sum of 5d. per score. Pedestrians did not pay, passing through a side gate.

Following the advent of railways and the consequent disappearance of stagecoaches and other traffic from the roads, the use of toll bars generally declined. At the close of the 19th century some eleven hundred turnpike trusts throughout the country had ceased to exist. The Brough -South Newbald Holmes Turnpike Trust had struggled on until 1872 when it was eventually closed. The Beverley and Hessle Turnpike Trust also closed two years later.

The passing of this trust as with the majority of other trusts

HULL AND CAVE NEW COACH.

R. J. CHAFFER

RESPECTFULLY informs his Friends and the Public, that he has this day commenced running a New Four-Inside Post-Coach, which leaves the White Hart, North Cave, every Morning (Sundays excepted) at a Quarter-past Seven, and the Fox and Coney, South Cave, at a Quarter before Eight; calls at the Half-Moon, Brantingham,—Green Dragon, Welton, —Duke of Cumberland, Ferriby,—and the Granby Inn, Hessle,—and arrives at Mr. Lyon's, the Black Horse, Carr-lane, at Half-past Nine; from whence it returns each Afternoon at a Quarter-past Four. Passengers and Parcels will meet with every attention, at each of the above places, and also at R. J. C.'s Posting and Coaching Establishment, Silvester-street, where every information relative to the different Coaches leaving Hull may be obtained.

R. J. C. begs to return his sincere thanks for the liberal encouragement he has received since his commencement, and trusts that his future exertions will secure to him a continuance; and hopes that the above Coach and arrangement will prove to be that accommodation so long wanted, NO COACH HAVING HITHERTO RUN BETWEEN NORTH CAVE AND HULL.

The above advertisement dated Monday, 4th May 1835 was in direct opposition to Miles' Coach, pulled not by horses but by cattle which operated between South Cave and Hull. Owing to the appalling state of the roads at that time and the poor condition of the cattle, it is recorded that four hours were sometimes consumed in the journey of 14 miles. Interestingly, this coach carried three classes of passenger; first, those who rode all the way; second, those who walked up the hills, and third, those who pushed the coach when a hill was encountered. By 1840, four coaches were passing through South Cave and returning daily including the "True Briton" to Selby and the "Mail" to Sheffield, both coaches stopping at the Fox and Coney. Also, the "Eclipse" to Wakefield and the "King William" to Hull both of which stopped at the Bear Inn.

throughout the country was not mourned since public opinion had long despised having to pay to travel on the roads. The cost of toll charges often meant considerable time would be spent by travellers prior to a journey endeavouring to find which route would entail the least expense by way of toll charges, the journey often covering a longer distance than would have been the case had none existed.

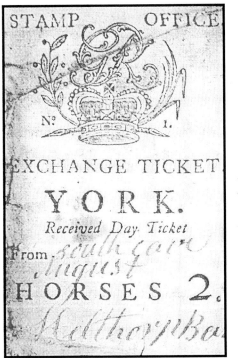

Left, a day ticket issued at the Kettlethorpe Bar, (demolished sometime after 1930), which, with the Brough Bar, came under the administration of the Brough Ferry-South Newbald Holmes Turnpike Trust. The original toll bar and house stood at the junction with the Beverley Road but were moved to a new site close by in the 1850s. The nearby Swinescaife Road was once the old toll road to Hull. Reproduced from the original by kind permission of the East Riding of Yorkshire County Council Archive Services, Beverley.

Right, a 19th century milestone attached to an older two step mounting block, in Westgate, North Cave. The milestone dates from the turnpiking of the road through Everthorpe and North Cave authorised by the Turnpike Act of 1774.

TURNPIKE TOLLS TO LET.

NOTICE is hereby given, that the TOLLS arising at the several TOLL GATES, upon the Turnpike Roads from BROUGH FERRY to SOUTH NEWBALD HOLMES, in the East-riding of the county of York, and from BROUGH to WELTON, in the said Riding, and called or known by the several names of KETTLETHORP GATE and BROUGH GATE, will be LET by AUCTION, to the best Bidder, at the house of BARNARD COOK, Innholder, in South Cave, in the said county of York, on Monday the Twenty-first day of April next, between the hours of Twelve and Two o'clock in the afternoon, in the manner directed by the Act passed in the Thirteenth Year of the Reign of His Majesty King George the Third, for regulating the Turnpike Roads, which TOLLS are to be Let at the clear Annual Rents following, viz.:—

KETTLETHORP BAR....................£60
BROUGH BAR.........................90

And will be put up at these Sums respectively.

Whoever happens to be the best Bidder, must at the same time give Security with sufficient Sureties, to the satisfaction of the Trustees of the said Turnpike Roads, for Payment of the Rent agreed for, and at such times as they shall direct.— Dated this 18th day of March, 1817.

JOHN ROBINSON,
South Cave, March 19, 1817.   Clerk to the said Trustees.

At first, many trustees appointed their own toll collectors, at a salary of about £10 per annum for being on duty for up to 16 hours per day. As this system was so unpopular, difficult to manage and open to a great deal of fraud, " Letting the tolls" soon took its place. This meant the right of toll collection was put up for auction to the highest bidder, who thus became the 'farmer' of the tolls at one or more of the trusts' tollgates. Toll farmers were speculators hoping to make a handsome profit. After paying the trustees, thereby giving a trust an assured income, and the wages of the toll collector he employed, the toll farmer could keep the subsequent balance himself. Left, in March 1817 the Fox and Coney, South Cave was the venue for this particular public auction of turnpike tolls.

The vast majority of farmers had their own horses and traps which they drove to market and most other people relied on the carriers for transporting goods. The carrier had a horse and cart and twice a week on Tuesday and Friday he would travel to Mytongate, Hull, where he would park near the market together with other carriers who travelled in from many of the outlying villages of Hull. There was a brisk business of buying and selling conducted around these carriers' carts. Butter, cheese, eggs, ducks and fowls, fruit and vegetables among other things would rapidly change hands. Towns people would arrive and request their parcels which had been sent from the rural areas and country people would present parcels for carriage and delivery as well as perhaps getting a ride back to their village. Here we see Robert

Donkin one of a number of carriers in the South Cave area, standing with his wagon outside the old shop at number 13, West End, South Cave. From the scene it appears he has just delivered a large crate.

Left, the existence of a wharf at Crabley Creek on the River Humber at Cave Sands is on record since at least 1787. Up until the opening of the Hull to Selby Railway in 1840 most farm produce went by cart from the Cave villages to Crabley Creek and was transported from there up the estuary. Considerable quantities of corn purchased from the South Cave markets were also shipped from here up the river and via the inland waterways to many towns in the West Riding of Yorkshire.

Right, the annual Sunday School outing from South Cave. This photograph taken at Riplingham crossroads in June 1921 shows a crowded wagonette with its horses especially decorated for the occasion. Until the era of the charabanc, outings were usually organised to somewhere relatively nearby, often to Woodale or Beverley Westwood. Occasionally, trips were arranged to seaside resorts such as Bridlington or Hornsea and farmers loaned wagons or rullies to take the children to Brough railway station.

Left, a horse-drawn sleigh used by Mr. Walter Scott, a grocer in Market Place, South Cave. The sleigh was used both for pleasure and to deliver goods to customers during the harsh winter of 1907.

Right, Dr. Robert D. Cameron of North Cave owned one of the earliest cars in the area. His chauffeur Mr. Swain is seen here at North Cave railway station awaiting his passengers.

Left, here we see a rather more modest vehicle, but early motoring was still only for the very wealthy. One of the cheapest cars in 1911 for example, was a small Rover costing £147, which was then a large sum of money and the upkeep of any car was costly. Here are members of the Goodwill family with their car parked outside number 50, Church Street, South Cave.

Right, waiting for help to arrive! This unfortunate accident shows a two-seat Briton open tourer which skidded off the road and into the beck near Frog Hall, in the West End of South Cave. It is believed that the photograph was taken in 1919 and that the driver was Mr. G. Laverack, a farmer from Drewton.

Rubber tyres made motoring more comfortable, but they also churned up the dust in great clouds, and this together with the increase in the volume of traffic caused the roads to show signs of breaking up. A National Road Board was set up in 1909, which advocated the spraying of roads with hot tar and the use of tarmacadam. This not only reduced the dust but gave smoother roads and fewer punctures. In the above photograph taken in 1933 are Donny Gibson and Jack Harvett with the steam roller which followed the tar sprayer. Jack, who was from Woodmansey near Beverley, used to travel around with his steam roller, towing a caravan in which he lived. From Sunday to Friday night he always parked on the green at Hotham. Alf Adamson remembers that in 1937 he took a job with his horse Prince, pulling the tar boiler cart around the streets of North Cave, Hotham and Newport for £1 per day. He recalls that it was a very hard job because he was usually placed down wind so the men at the rear, spreading the chippings, had no tar spray blowing onto them. As a result, the fumes caused his face to burn badly, and sometimes he would come home at night choking after the day's work . Alf made two holes in a brown paper bag and wore it over his head and put a sack over his horse's head to try and alleviate the terrible dust and fumes. Below can be seen the tar boiler and workers laying tarmac in Westgate, North Cave.

Above, Carlo Pratti's ice-cream van in Everthorpe Lane. Fred Barlow remembers that the van would often call round the North Cave area. On the right Fred aged 6 years and his elder brother Frank are seen here buying ice-cream in 1925.

Following the end of the Great War of 1914-18, motorcars became more readily available. Henry Ford, an American, led the way in the mass production of less expensive cars. His Model T. Ford was tremendously successful and placed motorcars within the reach of many ordinary people. Left, is a picture of Holt's bus in the 1920s which was a Model T. Ford with 14 seats. The bus could be converted into a carriers van by removing the body shell. Henry Jackson of West End, South Cave operated a Model T. Ford bus which was used for taking the South Cave village football team to away matches, the silver band and their instruments to events, and for general organised trips. On Saturday mornings, Henry used his bus to transport horse-meat to Hull Docks for Harry Rispin of Church Street, North Cave. The bus would be thoroughly cleaned out on his return ready for an afternoon excursion.

Travel of any great distance for pleasure was not to be enjoyed by ordinary people until the arrival of the brake or charabanc. A French word which translates as "carriage with benches," it was pronounced by English folk as "sharrabang." Local historian Archie Trout commented in his diary in July 1920 that, "Motor charabancs are a great boon, but their increase of numbers on Sundays is leading to a general increase of Sabbath desecration, which is to be regretted." A few years later tour buses became a common sight around the

Cave villages. During the summer months touring buses often parked outside the Fox and Coney, Market Place, South Cave, in readiness to take various groups out on day trips into the countryside or to the seaside as depicted on the right.

Above, Bob Thornham's coal lorry. Bob operated from South Cave railway station as did T. B. and A. J. Davis coal merchants of Church Street. Bob's round took in a number of local villages including Ellerker, Elloughton and Brough, whilst the Davis brothers concentrated more on the Cave villages and around the Newbald area. In c.1956 Bob gave up his business and joined his brothers Eric and Ron who were pig farming at Church Hill, West End, South Cave.

Left, this photograph was taken c.1959 in Station Road, North Cave and shows Mr. Albert Woodall's horse and milk cart with helpers. From the left, Susan Sharman, Jackie Oxtoby and Shelia Clark. The girls were given 3d. per week for helping to deliver the milk. Albert operated his business from "The Priory" 20, Newport Road. He originally had a milk round in Hull c.1930 but bought Mr. Harrison's North Cave round after he retired. His brother-in-law Stan Hardwick operated another milk round which Albert also purchased, that covered nearby Newport and Gilberdyke. Albert retired in the early 1960s.

Colonel William Henton Carver of North Cave was Member of Parliament for the Howdenshire District for 26 years. He was also a director of The London North Eastern Railway and was given the honour of having this steam engine named after him during the early 1950s.

South Cave railway station which opened in 1885 was situated one and a half miles to the north of the village. In the heyday of the railway, goods and coal trains would be passing through the station day and night.

South Cave and North Cave Railway Stations

The opening of the Hull to Selby Railway in 1840 proved to be a major improvement in transport facilities for the area. A number of proposals had been made to connect the Cave villages with this railway but none was implemented. Among these was the 1847 proposal for a railway to run between Hull and Market Weighton, via Brough.

One strong objector to this particular venture was the Reverend Edward Stillingfleet, the vicar of South Cave, who vehemently opposed the building of a railway station in the village. In writing to the Chairman of the proposed railway he commented,

"I have just cause to complain of Sunday evil at the public houses here and had we a railway, I have little doubt bad would be made worse. The scum of Hull would make it one place for their Sunday revels."

It was not until the advent of the Hull, Barnsley and West Junction Railway in 1885 that both North Cave and South Cave gained a direct access to the national railway network. This resulted in both freight and passenger traffic becoming much faster and more efficient.

This was the last substantial and independent new railway built in Great Britain. It was opened in 1885 with considerable help from Hull Corporation, in an effort to break the monopoly of the North Eastern Railway. However, the difficulties encountered in having to cut through the southern part of the chalk Wolds was grossly underestimated and costs soared. The final cost of the 53 miles of track laid between Hull and Barnsley was £9,500,000 equivalent to £179, 245 per mile, making it one of the most expensive railways ever constructed in this country.

The line never actually reached Barnsley but instead linked the Alexandra Dock, Hull, with Cudworth, near Barnsley, where it connected with the Midland Railway. There was a passenger service from Cannon Street Station in Hull to Cudworth but it only ever formed a small part of the company's operations.

The Hull and Barnsley Railway served mainly as a two-way freight system bringing coal from the West Yorkshire coalfields to Hull and the docks, with wool from Australia and Scandinavian timber being hauled in the opposite direction.

Despite what appeared to be a successful freight business the demise of this railway could be seen as early as 1st April 1912, when the North Eastern and the Hull and Barnsley companies combined. As predicted, the North Eastern company began taking the freight traffic from the smaller line.

Furthermore, by 1932 as a result of the continual lack of patronage, all passenger services west of Howden were withdrawn although the passenger service between South Howden and Hull was maintained. It provided a good service of ten passenger trains per day in each direction for the populations of Howden, North Cave, South Cave and Willerby.

With the increasing competition from bus companies and the growth in private motoring it was finally decided by the company to withdraw all passenger services between Howden and Hull with effect from the 1st August 1955. This occurred despite protests from local people, parish and rural councils as well as farming representatives.

Virtually the whole of the line was closed to freight traffic in 1958. The last through freight train into Hull on Saturday, 29th November of that year marked the end of 73 years of coal haulage over the Wolds. The line officially closed on the 6th April 1959 leaving only a pickup goods train serving Willerby and Little Weighton. This pickup service continued until the complete closure of the line in 1964.

Above, this view of North Cave railway station was taken on 3rd April 1959 by Neville Stead. Although local passenger trains on this section had ceased to run some four years earlier, the platform canopies are only just in the process of demolition. The railway bridge nearby was removed about 1985. Following the closure of the line the station buildings were used as a washing machine depot and then later for light industry before Mr. and Mrs. Leslie Cooper bought the property in 1964 and converted it into their home. During the 1970s a local doctor bought it and the "Booking Hall", as the property had been named, served as both a residence and surgery. The property is now a private residence.

Right, a notice advertising the closure of passenger services in 1955. A Stock Fund with public membership was founded in 1968 to purchase, restore and maintain examples of rolling stock belonging to the Hull and Barnsley West Junction Railway. Below, this wagon built in 1886, is now preserved together with other examples at Goathland on the North York Moors Railway which runs from Pickering to Grosmont.

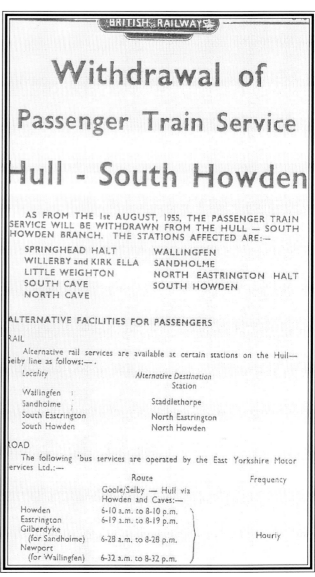

BRITISH RAILWAYS

Withdrawal of
Passenger Train Service
Hull - South Howden

AS FROM THE 1st AUGUST, 1955, THE PASSENGER TRAIN SERVICE WILL BE WITHDRAWN FROM THE HULL — SOUTH HOWDEN BRANCH. THE STATIONS AFFECTED ARE:—

SPRINGHEAD HALT	WALLINGFEN
WILLERBY and KIRK ELLA	SANDHOLME
LITTLE WEIGHTON	NORTH EASTRINGTON HALT
SOUTH CAVE	SOUTH HOWDEN
NORTH CAVE	

ALTERNATIVE FACILITIES FOR PASSENGERS

RAIL

Alternative rail services are available at certain stations on the Hull—Selby line as follows:—.

Locality	Alternative Destination Station
Wallingfen	
Sandholme	Staddlethorpe
South Eastrington	North Eastrington
South Howden	North Howden

ROAD

The following 'bus services are operated by the East Yorkshire Motor Services Ltd.:—

	Route	Frequency
	Goole/Selby — Hull via Howden and Caves:—	
Howden	6-10 a.m. to 8-10 p.m.	
Eastrington	6-19 a.m. to 8-19 p.m.	
Gilberdyke (for Sandholme)	6-28 a.m. to 8-28 p.m.	Hourly
Newport (for Wallingfen)	6-32 a.m. to 8-32 p.m.	

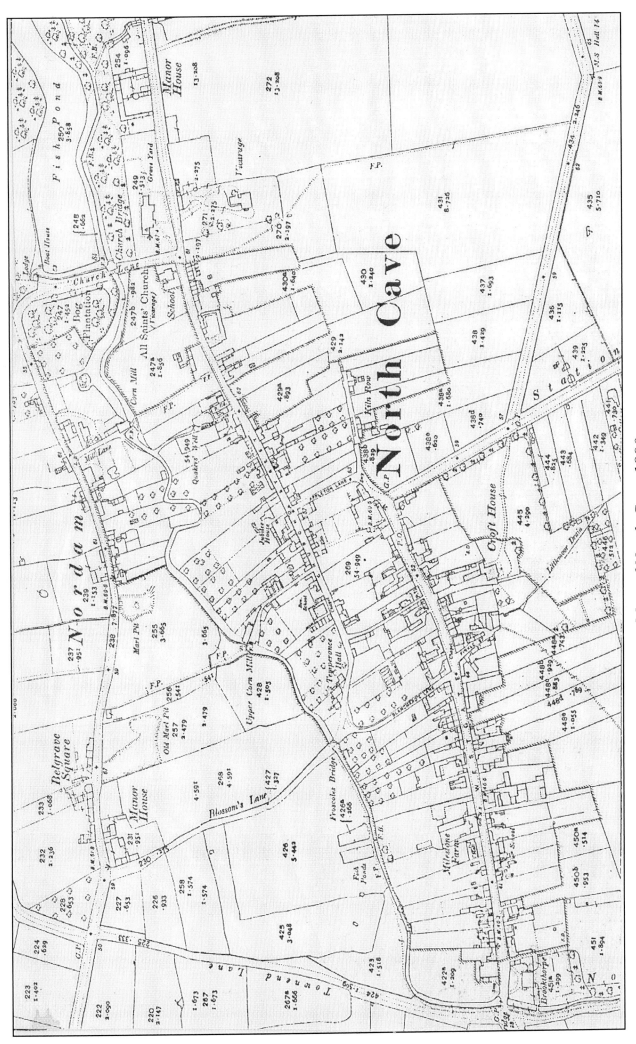

Map of North Cave 1890

105

Development of North Cave

The village of North Cave is situated at a distance of two-and-a-half miles from Market Place, South Cave and is the smaller and probably the more rural of the two villages. Like South Cave and the nearby hamlet of Everthorpe, there exists signs of very early settlement.

One of the largest inhabited sites, dating back about 2,000 years was discovered during quarrying operations at Dryham Lane in the village and was first excavated in 1974-1976. Archaeologists revealed the remains of a series of Iron Age hut circles overlain by a Romano-British aisled building with an associated drove road and field system which covered a four acre site.

When a further dig was carried out in the mid 1980s by the archaeology unit of the Humberside County Council's Architects Department, artefacts dating back even further to 3,500 BC (the last period of the Stone Age), were discovered.

Under the direction of Mr. John Dent a number of items were found. These included an arrowhead, a scraper for cleaning animal skins, a chisel or drilling tool and a fine axe with the blade sharpened by rubbing with sandstone.

In addition hundreds of Iron Age and Roman relics were unearthed which indicated that the site had been a former hamlet dependent mainly on farming. It was Mr. Dent's opinion that the sands and gravels around North Cave were extensively farmed by the native population both before and after the Roman conquest in A.D. 71.

It was concluded that these early farmers may have used some of their time making iron from local stone because the remains of slag found over the excavated area pointed to the existence of at least one iron smelting furnace in the settlement which had continued to be used during the Roman occupation period and until about A.D. 300.

Little is known of the early economic or social development of the village itself. However, it is mentioned in the Domesday Book, compiled for William the Conqueror in 1066 which refers to the village as, *"... another Cave."* Like its neighbour South Cave the village name North Cave is believed to have been derived from the Anglian word 'caf' which was used to describe a stream or beck. Land owners in 1066, in and around North Cave included Robert Malet and the Count Mortain.

During the 12th century pious gifts of local land and property were made by noblemen to the Church. For example, Roger Hay gave one mill and its income to the brothers of the Hospital of St. Peter's (later St. Leonards Hospital) and Roger de Mowbray gave 65 acres of land in North Cave to the monks of St. Mary of Byland.

Another North Cave estate belonging to John Stather had been donated to the Priory of St. Andrew the Apostle in Nether Acaster, near York but was later confiscated by the Crown during the dissolution of the monasteries by King Henry VIII in 1536.

In 1553 the Reverend John Nowell, the Vicar of Giggleswick, North Yorkshire and a chaplain to King Edward VI, (son of Henry VIII and under whose reign the suppression of the monasteries continued), persuaded the King to endow the confiscated North Cave estate and its annual income from tenants to the Grammar School at Giggleswick. Consequently, the grant of a Royal Charter shortly followed in May of that year and the Grammar School remained one of the largest landowners at North Cave for almost 400 years; the estate being sold in 1921.

During the Middle Ages, the Metham family of Metham near Howden, amassed a large estate in North Cave which included land in nearby Everthorpe and Drewton. When North Cave was enclosed by an Act of Parliament in 1765, Sir George Montgomery Metham was awarded 442 acres. The enclosing of the once open

Archaeologist John Dent reveals one of two Iron Age pits found on the Dryham Lane site. This remarkable photograph shows this particular pit to be have been wicker lined. It is believed to have been originally designed like this in order to separate clear water from sand and gravel, thus enabling the villagers' buckets to be filled all year round with clean water. Settlement was possible on this low lying land because it was just above the water table and this has helped to preserve wood and other organic remains found on the site.

fields meant that the old method of strip farming (which had been considered wasteful of time and labour), gave way to compact farms and better agricultural practice.

Wallingfen situated to the west of the village was a vast area of marshy common grazing land. Although drainage began in the 13th century it was not until 1772 that a main drainage channel was constructed making Wallingfen much more productive. Shortly after this improvement the land was enclosed in 1777.

Much of the village lies along Westgate and Church Street and many of the buildings including several farmhouses date back to the 18th and 19th centuries. The North Cave Beck gently meanders slightly to the north before turning sharply to flow beneath Westgate at Townend Bridge in the direction of South Cave. Three mills were once powered by the waters of the Beck. The integral northern area of the village is known as Nordham. Today, North Cave has a population of around 1,400 boosted by some new housing developments which have taken place in recent years. Certain parts of the village were designated as conservation areas in 1974.

Station Road

Above, looking towards the old North Cave railway station bridge (now demolished), from the corner of Everthorpe Lane. Along this road known as Station Road, over 100 council houses have been erected since the Second World War. Quite a number of them stand on Fairfield, a site just before the bridge and on the left in this picture. The annual Cave Fair was often held on Fairfield on Trinity Saturday and Monday every year up until the First World War. A spring sale conducted by Messrs Tuton and Tuton, auctioneers was also held for many years on this site. Farmers would bring livestock and surplus agricultural implements and machinery to this event which finally ceased in the 1950s.

North Cave was on the route of the Hull and Barnsley West Riding Junction Railway which opened in 1885. A railway station was opened here in the same year but the gradual decline in rail traffic led to the final closure of the line in 1964, several years after the last passenger train passed through North Cave. Here we see the front entrance of the station taken in 1904 during its heyday. The main station building is now a private residence.

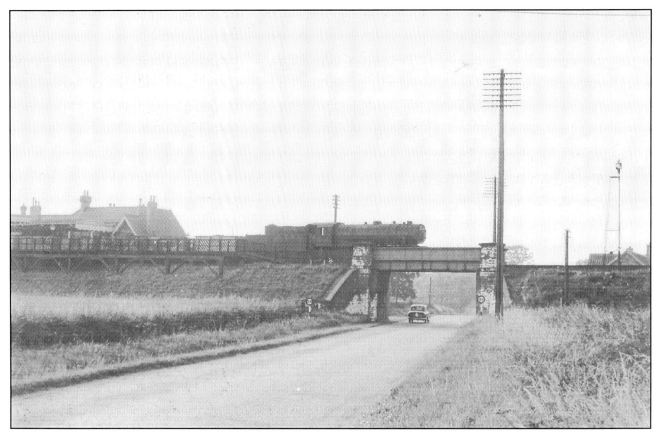

Above, this photograph taken by J. Oxley shows the Station Road Bridge which was dismantled in 1985. Prior to its demolition all East Yorkshire Motor Service buses on the North Cave route were made with flat roofs in order that they could negotiate the low bridge. Mary Mason, a conductress for the company during the 1940s, recalls that if the wrong bus was sent from the depot the bus driver would have to divert the bus via Everthorpe village to get into North Cave.

An aerial view of Station Road and the junction with Westgate taken c.1970.

This photograph taken in 1929 shows the war memorial on the right and in the background Mr. C. Anderson & Son's garage. The building once formed part of William Saunder's foundry business which had flourished throughout the 19th century until c.1918 when it closed. It reopened shortly afterwards as a garage which was demolished in 1937 to make way for a pair of semi-detached almshouses built by the Carver family. Opposite the foundry was a row of old cottages known as Kiln Row. The photographs below were taken in 1974 and show some of the Kiln Row cottages in a derelict state. Later that year the cottages were finally demolished. A sheltered housing scheme consisting of 34 flats built in 1993 now stands on the site.

Right, No. 1, Kiln Row, was the former home of Ernest Harrison and his family. Above, a view of the front of Nos. 4 and 5, Kiln Row. The cottage at No. 2, was last occupied by Tom Donkin, No. 3, by Mr. Beverley, No. 4, by Mr. Taylor and No. 5, by Miss Lundy.

Westgate

The large grey-brick house known as 'The Croft' is thought to have replaced an earlier property which was quite probably a farmhouse. It was built c.1875 by Richard Petch, a local farmer and butcher. It has been the home of the Carver family since 1895 when William Henton Carver bought the property and came to live in it with his new wife, Florence. He was in the 3rd King's Own Yorkshire Light Infantry for 17 years, retiring in 1908, but on the outbreak of the Great War he raised the 10th Service Battalion of the East Yorkshire Regiment and served in Egypt and France until 1919. William held many positions in his life, among them Member of Parliament for Howdenshire for19 years. His son John Henton Carver married Juliet Gurney in 1932,

heiress to the Hotham Hall estate. They came to live at The Croft in 1961, following the death of William. Their son Peter inherited The Croft as well as the 1,300 acre Hotham estate in 1969. The Carver family have been prominent in raising money for various charities. In 1987 the centenary year of the St. John Ambulance organisation Peter and his wife Jacky held a Grand Charity Ball set in an elegant marquee in the grounds of The Croft. Almost 500 people attended the Ball, including the main guest, H.R.H. Princess Margaret, Grand President of the St. John Ambulance Association and Brigade. The event

raised over £25,000 for the St. John Humberside Appeal, which was used to re-equip the county's brigade.

H.R.H. Princess Margaret is seen in this photograph with Peter Carver about to sign the visitors' book at The Croft in October 1987.

Here we see the North Cave and Hotham Boy Scouts in 1910. This was the first patrol of Boy Scouts in the district and was formed in connection with the Church Lads' Brigade, in September 1909. Only boys attending the church or Sunday School, between the ages of 10 and 16 years were eligible for membership. It appears that the patrol had disbanded by 1914 as a result of the onset of the First World War. In fact, the majority of the boys seen here would have fought in that war. Another troop of scouts, with John Carver as Scoutmaster was formed on 7th July 1924 with eight

boys. A further eight joined shortly afterwards and the troop flourished for many years. In 1926 the troop was formally presented to H.R.H. Edward Prince of Wales during his stay at Hotham Hall. The Prince presented the scouts with a flag which today is kept in All Saints' Church, North Cave. John Carver's son Peter has also been Humberside Scout Commissioner but stepped down in 1990, although he remains the County President of the Humberside Scout Association.

Herbert S. Parkinson,

Agricultural Auctioneer
and Valuer.

North Cave, - Hull.

During the 1890s and until c.1925 the Parkinson family ran an auctioneer and valuer's business from their home at Sand Hall on Station Road, North Cave. In 1913 another auctioneer John William Tuton opened a similar business in the village.

A village school with a master's house was built in 1770 on land donated by Sir George Montgomery Metham, the Lord of the Manor. However, in 1823 a new Boys' Church School was opened further down Westgate and in nearby Church Street a Girls' School was built in 1831. It is not known when the original village school was demolished but two modern properties at 6a and 6b Westgate now stand on the former site. Above, a notice placed in the Hull Advertiser dated 1811 requesting applications for the vacancy of Schoolmaster.

The small single storey building on the left of centre was once the site of the village post office. In 1879 Frederick Taylor a grocer and tailor was also operating a postal service from there which was described as "Money Order, Telegraph and Savings Bank Office." Mrs. Mary Taylor was postmistress and shopkeeper in 1892 and was succeeded in 1909 by her daughter Miss Rose Taylor. Older villagers recall Frank Clarke who although almost blind, worked for Rose, delivering telegrams and newspapers around North Cave and as far as Hotham Carrs. He was known as the village errand lad and as he wore wooden clogs, could be heard as well as seen as he pushed his wheelbarrow round the streets. Using his barrow he was able to move items of furniture or anything else that needed transporting. The post office moved to new premises in 1937 situated further down Westgate and the business was taken over by Mrs. Mabel Allison who was the postmistress for many years. The old post office premises became Barlow's electrical shop and today is Peacock and Granville's Estate Agency.

On the corner of Westgate and Station Road stands Morton's Funeral Services. For many years the Saunders family had a joinery shop here where horse-drawn wooden ploughs were made. Alf Adamson of Hotham remembers that he was the last person to buy a plough which cost £1.17s.6d, before Saunders shut down in 1938. Mr. Len Johnson then started a garage business from the premises. The business changed hands twice before John Barnett Morton purchased it in 1975 and opened it as a funeral service. Right, Stan Hardwick is seen here in 1981 with a Saunders wooden plough. These were always painted red. Hicks Foundry in Church Street also made ploughs but in iron which were always painted blue.

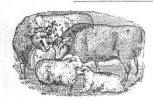

J. H. GRAY,
Family Butcher,
NORTH CAVE

Nothing but the BEST supplied.

Above, looking westwards towards the Methodist Chapel on the corner of Finkle Street. To the right is the old Albion public house and before it Glebe House an 18th century stone built property. To the extreme left of the foreground of this view taken in 1905 is No. 5, Westgate where John. H. Gray had a butchers shop. Further along at No. 9, was Robert Ernest Parkinson's shop. He had a variety of occupations including cobbler, saddler and hairdresser. One other cobbler in the village during the 1920s-30s was Tom Blacker of Church Street. His grandson Jack Blacker recalls that he would often be sent round the village after school to deliver mended shoes to customers.

Left, looking eastwards towards Mr. A. E. Scotts' grocery shop. A large number of local children pose for this photograph taken c.1905.

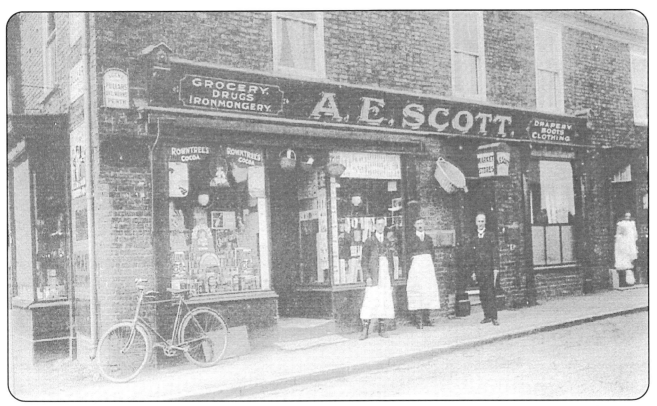

Above, from c.1860-1915, Scott's grocery, hardware and drapery business was the main shop in the village. Mr. Anthony Eland Scott is seen here on the left with his two sons Eland and Raymond. Mr. Scott was instrumental among farmers and businessmen in the area in the setting up of the North Cave and District Fire Association fire service in 1866. The fire engine itself was a Merryweather manual and was used to fight mainly agricultural fires. Cave Castle at South Cave was saved twice by the intervention of the brigade. The fire service later came under the auspices of the North Cave Parish Council and continued in existence until just before the First World War. The engine was kept for some years on the premises of Saunders and Hicks, Ironfounders and Blacksmiths, in Church Street. Mr. Hicks was the captain of the brigade and one of six voluntary firemen. During the First World War, Mr. Scott and his sons moved to new smaller premises further down the street where they sold mainly drapery and hardware. Uriah Botham from Hessle took over the old shop. The Bothams sold their own meats, cakes and bread and prided themselves on selling only the best quality provisions.

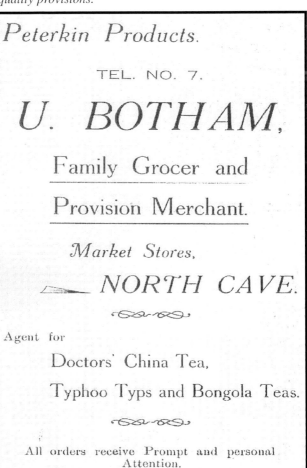

The White Horse public house was in existence in 1823 but had become known as the Albion by 1864. Joseph Foster and his family came to the Albion in 1908. As well as being a publican Joseph was also a horse dealer and breaker. Horses would be brought by their owners to be broken in the yard at the back of the premises. He was landlord until his death in 1918, after which his wife Fanny took on the licence until her retirement in 1940. Mrs. Foster is seen here outside the Albion c.1920. One of her sons, William, then became licensee until 1948. After this date it changed hands a few times before it ceased business in 1971 and became a curio shop. It later became the Sundial Restaurant owned and run by Jane Marsden. The former public house is now owned by Mr. and Mrs. Phil Cockin who run their Penny Farthing Antiques shop, as well as a bed and breakfast business from the premises.

The White Hart was built in 1776 as a private house. It was later bought by James Pinkerton, an engineer working on the Market Weighton canal. By the late 18th century the building had become a coaching inn known as the White Hart. During the 1840s the premises were also used as a posting house. In 1872 publican Richmond Cousens who was also a farmer began a weekly corn market which continued until just before the First World War. Only a narrow passageway separated the White Hart from its neighbour the Albion. Many villagers remember David Hart, publican at the White Hart, during the 1930-40s. At the bottom of the pub yard he kept a dairy herd and had a milk round in the village. Milk would be taken round on a three wheeled tricycle which had a big frame built on to the front and in which the churns were carried. Mr. Hart would give the village children a penny each at Christmas and a duck or goose egg at Easter. After he retired from the White Hart he opened a cobblers shop on the corner of Finkle Street, Westgate.

HULL AND LONDON COACH,
EVERY DAY.

THE Proprietors of the RODNEY COACH return their sincere thanks to the public at large, for past favours; and now beg leave to acquaint them, that they intend to RUN the same EVERY DAY, from the 10th of June instant; and humbly solicit a continuance of their patronage and support.

The Rodney Coach will set off from the BULL and SUN INN, MYTON-GATE, HULL, EVERY NIGHT at half past eleven o'clock, by way of North Cave, Howden, Booth-Ferry, Thorne, and Doncaster, where it meets the HIGH FLYER COACH; and arrives at the WHITE HORSE, FETTER-LANE, LONDON, at one o'clock the next day.—Sets out from London every morning at seven, and arrives at Hull the following evening.

This Coach does not sleep on the road, avoids the dangerous passage of the Humber, and is thirty miles nearer than by way of York.

The FARE.

Inside to London,	£3 10—Outside,	£1 18
Inside to Doncaster,	1 3—Outside,	0 14

PERFORMED BY
JOHN MORRIS, Hull,
THOMAS WALKER, North Cave,
WILLIAM WELLS, Booth-Ferry,
THOMAS VAUSE, Thorne,
And, the PROPRIETORS of the HIGH FLYER COACH.

N. B. The Rodney Coach meets at the Black Boy Inn, Doncaster, the Sheffield, Buxton, Manchester, Derby, Birmingham, and Bristol Coach, from whence Passengers and Parcels are forwarded every Day, to all parts of the West of England.

*** The Proprietors will not be accountable for any Bag, Parcel or Truss, of any description, above the value of Five Pounds, except entered as such, and paid for accordingly.

An advertisement dated 1823 for the "Rodney" Coach Service, which used to call at the White Hart coaching house on its journey from Hull to Thorne to meet the "High Flyer" Coach to London.

This photograph, taken in the 1940s, shows the village post office on the immediate right. R. E. Lilley's butchers shop at No. 24, Westgate was just beyond it. The butchers shop formed part of a late 17th century house.

R. E. LILLEY
PORK BUTCHER
EASTRINGTON ... NORTH CAVE
Waterworks Street, HULL, and also
Market Hall, HULL.
AT EACH OF OUR SHOPS AT THE ABOVE ADDRESSES
WILL BE FOUND THE CHOICEST OF
Pork and Pork Products, Sausages,
Joints of Pork, Pies, Brawn.
WE WELCOME YOUR ENQUIRIES, AND ARE CERTAIN
THAT WE CAN GIVE YOU SATISFACTION. JOIN THE
RANKS OF THE WISE AND SHOP AT ONE OR OTHER OF
" LILLEY'S " SHOPS.

On the right-hand side of this photograph are Nos. 32 and 34, Westgate, which were erected in 1863 by Charles Greenwood, builder. A fellmonger's house with outbuildings and a yard had formerly occupied the site and Peter Blanchard is listed as fellmonger here in 1841. James Stather, his son-in-law continued the business here until 1863 when the site was demolished. The front of the old fellmonger's house, built of local stone was retained as the back wall of the two new houses, the front and sides which were built of brick. In an adjoining building Henry Holmes and his sons James and William manufactured rope and twine from 1840 until c.1855 when the two brothers

moved the business to the nearby village of Everthorpe. In addition William also became the landlord of the Duke of York public house. William returned to North Cave c.1871 and started a business selling flesh and bone manure but later changed his occupation to that of a coal merchant. Greenwood's building and contractors business continued until the 1950s. George Greenwood, (son of Harry Holmes Greenwood, bricklayer), who was crippled as a result of polio at the age of 7 ran a cobbler's shop from an old railway carriage in his garden at No. 32, Westgate. George was a well known character in the village and following his death in 1994 aged 82 years a wooden seat was placed in his memory by North Cave Parish Council on the little village green near Froscoles Bridge, a place much frequented by George in his later years.

William Holmes
Manufacturer
of
flesh and bone manure at £3.10s. per ton,
which is acknowledged to be the cheapest
and best in the market:

CART GREASE ALWAYS ON HAND

Right, William Blanshard was the local road sweeper. Following heavy rain, the beck would overflow, and in order to prevent flooding on the nearby main road, William was constantly clearing the drain tops further down the lane. After the beck springs were diverted to the Newbald reservoir, the problem of flooding was alleviated since the depth of the beck was considerably lowered. In recognition of William's faithful service the lane was renamed Blanshards Lane.

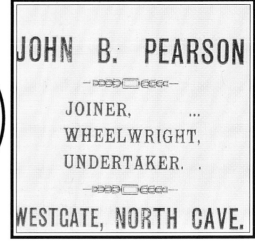

JOHN B. PEARSON

JOINER, ...
WHEELWRIGHT,
UNDERTAKER. .

WESTGATE, NORTH CAVE.

Looking down Westgate towards Townend Bridge. On the left was John B. Pearson's undertakers and wheelwright business. Further along on the right, Milestone Farm, an 18th century farmhouse can just be seen. An old mounting block with an attached milestone still stands against the front wall.

Since the late 1960s Pamela Hotham has toured the country from her Milestone Farm home, entertaining and teaching puppet-making to all age groups. Following a show, the Milestone Puppet Theatre's creator is often inundated with requests from schoolchildren asking how to make the latest television cartoon characters as well as the more traditional kings, wizards, witches and clowns. All the puppets are made from papier machè; discarded scraps of cloth, old spoons, hats, buttons and cartons. Pamela is seen here teaching some youngsters the art of puppetry early in her long career which still flourishes today. "It's marvellous fun," she says enthusiastically, "The children love it and I find it greatly rewarding. What other reasons do I need to continue?"

Billy Bond, another old character of North Cave earned his living during the winter by killing pigs and working on the land. He usually spent his time hedging during the summer months. Beryl Waddingham recalls, as a young girl on her way to school during the 1930s, often seeing the freshly killed pigs hanging up over the arch at No. 74, Westgate next to the house where Billy lived.

Above, the North Cave village hall was built c.1910 by Colonel J. B. Stracey-Clitherow of Hotham Hall.

Right, this photograph taken c.1910 outside Milestone Farm shows the village hall committee, which included William Henton Carver and his wife Florence. The hall was refronted and given to the parish as a gift by Juliet Carver, granddaughter of J. B. Stracey-Clitherow in the 1960s.

Right, James Anderson the village blacksmith is seen with one of his ten children, Frank, busy at the anvil. This photograph was taken in the forge in 1893 when James was 60 years of age. Apart from shoeing horses the Andersons would manufacture or repair articles for domestic and agricultural use. The blacksmiths business continued until Frank's death in 1962. Jessie Holmes remembers often visiting the old forge when she was a small child to watch her uncle Frank at work. The most fascinating objects to her were the pair of huge leather bellows used to keep the furnace alive and the many rows of horse shoes hung all over the walls and the beams of the forge.

Right, Martha Hall was born in North Cave on the 11th February 1850 and lived in the village all her life. Martha took the position of housekeeper to James Anderson the village blacksmith, following the death of his wife Mary in 1883. Four years later James and Martha married but tragically in 1896 their only son Freddie died of pneumonia at the age of 5 years and was buried in All Saints' churchyard. In her later years, Martha was affectionately known as "Granny Anderson". Her husband James died in 1919 aged 86 years but Martha lived on until 1955 having reached the remarkable age of 105 years. Martha lived with her stepson Frank in the house attached to the blacksmiths shop and she is seen here in 1954 aged 104 years with her cat Ginger. In her final years she was still very astute and in good health except for her eyesight which was beginning to fail. Martha, who had seen six monarchs on the throne, attributed her longevity to the fact that she never drank or smoked. A devout Methodist, she could be heard for two hours each evening singing in her rich contralto voice from her comprehensive repertoire of hymns.

Left, Brookthorpe formerly known as Low Hall, is an 18th century house reconstructed during the 19th century and stands in its walled grounds close to Townend Bridge. In 1808 a Maquis De Villedeuil was renting the property from a Thomas Wood who had to sell the hall at an auction at the White Hart in January that year, in order to repay a debt. It is said that the Maquis had escaped to England sometime during the French Revolution (1789-99). During the 'Reign of Terror' (Oct 1793- July 1794), about 1,400 opponents of the Jacobins led by Robespierre were executed, mainly by the guillotine.

Right, 'Pound Day' at Brookthorpe on Friday, 17th July 1912. The event was hosted by Dr. and Mrs. Robert D. Cameron to raise money for Dr. Barnado's Homes and the Rockcliffe Home for Blind Women in Hull. A string band was in attendance playing selections of music throughout the day.

Right, Bill Taylor an old character of North Cave could often be seen tenting cows in the lanes around the village's grass verges. He is shown here c.1920 near Townend Bridge with Low Hall in the background. Bill could often be found sitting under a large umbrella near the railway embankment while the cows grazed. Between April and October every year he would tent about 20 cows a week at 1/- per cow. Bill would save 5/- each week which he would use to live on during the winter. Townend Bridge was erected in 1885 and was altered and widened one hundred years later in 1985.

Above left, Newport Road c.1933. The old Hull and Barnsley West Junction Railway bridge is just visible in the distance. On the middle left of this view can be seen a block of semi-detached houses known as 'Brookvillas' which were built just after the First World War by Greenwoods, a local building firm. Above right, a closer view of the property taken c.1920.

Right, many older residents of North Cave remember John William Cade as quite a character in his time. Born in 1890 at Mill Farm, Everthorpe, John was brought up by his grandparents Alfred and Sarah Houseman. He moved to North Cave when he was 16 years old working a small-holding of 18 acres, which was situated in Crosslands Lane, off Dryham Lane, North Cave. He later purchased the small-holding for £200 from the owners, who ran the White Hart public house in Westgate, North Cave. In 1956, at the age of 66 years he built himself a new home on his land with timber which he had bought from exhibitors at an agricultural show held at Beverley. It took him three months to build his home, which consisted of a kitchen, two bedrooms and a coalhouse. He never married and this wooden shack remained his home for the rest of his life. John, as a young man occasionally worked for the Pearson family in Everthorpe, who were joiners and wheelwrights. For a period he was also a postman cycling 15 miles each day around the Broomfleet area. On the right, John seen with his dog Peggy. He died aged 93 years in 1983.

Left, this peculiar contraption attached to the tractor was known as the 'Rapidcut Hedge Trimmer' and was developed in 1949 by Jack Foster & Co., Agricultural Engineers, formerly of Newport Road. The company, which began c.1940, had originally manufactured parts for aircraft and was known as North Cave Components Ltd. The idea for the hedge trimmer had been developed from the 'horse-drawn hedge cutter' originally invented by Housemans of Leaming Bar. Fosters also manufactured the 'Sabre Scrub Clearer' which was just as it is described. These two products were contracted out all over the country together with Foster's employees. This publicity photograph taken at Rudston Walk Farm, near South Cave c.1950 shows Bob Bruce and Geoff Hardwick at the wheel. Geoff worked for the firm for a total of 11 years before becoming an engine fitter at the Blackburn Aircraft factory in Brough.

This photograph is a view looking up from Townend Bridge to Westgate and was taken c.1960. In it, on the left, can be seen Anderson's blacksmiths shop and house. Following Frank Anderson's death in 1962, the house, land, and blacksmiths shop were sold at auction. For a short while Walter Taylor sold cycles and sweets from an outbuilding before John Brian Holtby bought the premises in 1963. The old blacksmiths shop was demolished as well as the old building where Walter had sold his wares. The remaining

outbuildings were converted into a workshop for repairing cars. Mr. Holtby sold the business in 1987. Opposite Anderson's at number 73, Westgate, was Kate Gleadhill's shop. During the 1930s she had a caravan in the back garden of the shop from which she ran a cafe. Her daughter Greta later took over the shop and ran it for many years until her retirement.

Right, James Anderson father of James Anderson, jnr. who became the village blacksmith is seen here standing with his horse and carriers cart. Between 1845-49 he paid for young James to serve an apprenticeship to a blacksmith in nearby South Cave. This photograph was taken at the dawn of photography c.1838-40. It is thought to be the earliest photograph in existence of a scene from North Cave. As a carrier, James would travel with goods and passengers to and from Hull Market on Tuesdays and Fridays.

Above, Mr. Tom Denton was headmaster of the Boys' School in Westgate for some 39 years, retiring from the position in 1925. He is seen here with some of his pupils in 1908. The school was housed in part of an old Wesleyan Chapel purchased in 1840 by the Vicar of All Saints' Church, North Cave, Canon John Jarratt. In 1934 the Girls' School in Church Street was enlarged and became co-educational taking pupils from the Boys' School. The old school building was used as the Hotham and North Cave Home Guard Headquarters during the Second World War. The schoolmaster's house (now a private residence), survived, but the adjoining Boys' School was later demolished.

Above, shopkeeper Miss Emma Freda Chambers in 1971 shortly before she retired at the age of 67 years. Her general store at number 57, Westgate had been in the Chamber's family possession since c.1891 but had first opened c.1731. Miss Chambers, known as Freda, was born in 1904 in the house attached to the shop and until her retirement had lived there all her life. Freda moved to a bungalow at Eastfield in Station Road and lived there until she died in 1986 at the age of 82. No modernisation had ever been carried out on the premises and the small wooden drawer fittings seen in the background of this photograph would have originally been used to store herbs and loose foodstuffs. For many years Freda was very well known for her dance band 'Rio', which played at many venues in the district. Freda played the piano, Victor Pearson, violin, Bert Stather, drums and Cliff Leake, saxophone. Inset. A photograph of Freda's parents Thomas and Emma who ran the business before her.

Mr. George Bryant Hotchin's grocery store at number 21, Westgate in c.1910. Modern-day food regulations would not now allow this mouth-watering outdoor display of hams. George was known locally as 'Currant' Hotchin since some of his customers believed he would cut a currant in half in order to make up the correct weight. In the early 1920s he started a market gardening business in Church Street and the shop became Frederick Goode's grocery and drapery store. Earlier, in 1851, the premises had served as William Hewson's grocery store and a receiving house for post. Letters arrived at 8.10 am and were dispatched at 4.15 p.m. Robert Dalton Watson the village blacksmith was the next sub-postmaster and from 1857 was issuing Money Orders although he did not pay them. Inset. George "currant" Hotchin.

Left, Mr. Harold Sleight Mews opened a butchers shop in Westgate c.1897. Harold travelled round the area with his pony and cart delivering customers' orders. After he died in 1946, his wife Pearl converted the shop into a general hardware and drapery store. In 1955 their son Malcolm changed its use to an electrical appliances shop. The premises were demolished c.1990 and a new electrical shop was erected in its place by the Mews family.

Right, an Edwardian view of Westgate looking eastwards with Milestone Farm to the left and the former Boys' School to the right.

In November 1870 a new Primitive Methodist Chapel on the corner of Finkle Street was opened. Made of Newport brick, it cost £804 and incorporated a school room. It replaced an older chapel which had stood in Quaker Lane, Church Street. Following the Second World War there was a decline in membership in both the Wesleyan and the Primitive Societies and from 1960 the two Societies merged when the Wesleyan Centenary Chapel in Church Street closed. In 1989 following the discovery of dry rot and the need for extensive repairs, an ambitious project to modernise the Westgate Chapel was undertaken. The congregation held their meetings and services in the village hall until the work on the chapel was completed. On Saturday, 5th June 1993 the refurbished building was reopened for chapel and community use. There was once a pinfold situated against the chapel wall where the village pinder drove any straying animals. In order to reclaim them their owners were obliged to pay a fee.

Right, number 5, Finkle Street to the rear of the Westgate Chapel was built c.1765 to house the poor of the parish. In 1830 there were some 13 inmates, 8 from North Cave and others from Hotham and Blacktoft. The workhouse closed in 1839 following the erection of a new Union Workhouse in Howden. The Poor Law Union Act for Howden in 1837 required all parishes within the Poor Union to have one central workhouse to which each village was obliged to send its paupers.

This aerial view looking westwards along Church Street was taken c.1970. It was known in 1719 as Kirk Gate then later as High Street but by the mid-19th century it had become Church Street.

Manor Farm East and North Cave Hall

Manor Farm East was built during the 17th century although parts of the building date back to earlier times. The farm previously served the needs of North Cave Hall until 1773 when the residence was sold.

A central feature of the farm is an early 18th century octagonal dovecote. In the days before improved livestock breeding and fodder crops the birds provided the main winter meat for the landed gentry of North Cave Hall which stood immediately to the west of Manor Farm East.

On the far left of the farmhouse still exists a tithe-window which is reminiscent of the time when tithes, formerly a kind of payment in agricultural goods, were brought by the parishioners for the maintenance of the nearby All Saints' Church and its incumbent. Following the Tithe Commutation Act of 1836 tithes were abolished and replaced by payments of rent for land.

North Cave Hall was the home of the Metham family from the 16th century, but it was demolished soon after the estate was sold in 1773 by George Montgomery Metham, the last of his family line.

Legend has it that an underground passage once led from the former brewhouse situated in the far left hand block of Manor Farm East to the Hall. It is quite likely that this legend is true, although to date no traces of a tunnel have ever been found.

The evidence for the existence of a tunnel lies in the fact that the Metham family were staunch Roman Catholics in the reign of Queen Elizabeth I. During her reign (1558-1603), the Queen sought to enforce the protestant religion on all her subjects and those who resisted were harshly dealt with.

Sir Thomas Metham VIII (1526-72), was committed to York Castle dungeons for his Roman Catholic beliefs and following

This photograph taken in 1908 shows Manor Farm East then farmed by Ernest Suddaby. In the foreground can be seen a number of turkeys all fattened up for Christmas. By the end of the 19th century the turkey had taken over from the goose as the favoured Christmas bird. The large 18th century octagonal dovecote can be seen in the background.

several years of confinement in his cell he died there.

These dungeons lay below water-level and the more obstinate recusants often languished and perished there. Outside its walls many a priest suffered the barbarous ritual of a traitor's death, that of being hung, drawn and quartered.

His son Thomas Metham IX (1546 -1610), is recorded as having sheltered a priest at North Cave Hall in the late 16th century. The gentry were the chief supporters of the old Roman Catholic faith and North Cave Hall could well have been a key house where priests were continually in residence.

The Hall is assumed to have had a system of hiding places since the family took the risk of sheltering at least one priest there. However, the actual truth will never be known since the Hall was completely demolished by 1823 and no plans, drawings or anything visible remain of the building.

The Metham Family

The Metham family, of Metham, near Howden, became prominent landowners in the area during the middle-ages. The earliest record of their connection with North Cave is the existence of two alabaster figure monuments in All Saints' Church. These are of Sir Thomas Metham IX (1546-1610) and his wife Catherine (right), who were resident at the manor house, known as North Cave Hall which had previously stood to the east of the church.

Their son, Sir Thomas Metham X (1575-1644) obtained a grant from King Charles I, of a court leet and free warren in his Manor of North Cave, with liberty to enclose up to 500 acres for a park. A staunch royalist during the Civil Wars, Sir Thomas Metham X raised a regiment of Yorkshire volunteers which fought at Atherton Moor, Selby, Hull and Marston Moor near York. At the age of 69 years Sir Thomas was killed on Marston Moor on the 2nd July 1644 when the Royalists were defeated by Oliver Cromwell. His estates at Metham and North Cave passed to his widow Mary.

In 1646, following the death of Mary and with no direct male heir, the estates descended to their nephew George Metham (1618-72). George and his family, continued to live at the old moated grange at Metham until it fell into disrepair when they moved to North Cave Hall. His son George Metham II (1655-1716) bequeathed the estate to his son Philip Metham (1690-1732) who was the last male representative of the family. He died unmarried and without making a will in 1732. As a consequence his estate was divided equally between his two sisters, Dorothy and Barbara. Dorothy died unmarried in 1737. Barbara married Hugh Montgomery on the 23rd October 1713. Their son George on succeeding to his mother's estate in 1763 adopted her maiden name, Metham, in order to carry on the family connection.

George Montgomery Metham, however, embarked on a riotous and extravagant career in London and among other escapades ran away with a famous actress of the day, a Miss Bellamy. Indeed this sudden elopement caused her manager to announce from the stage that, *"The leading lady couldn't play because she had been carried off by Mr. Metham."* Nevertheless, he became Sheriff of Yorkshire in 1756 and was later knighted for his services. In 1757 he was a Member of Parliament for Hull.

During the 1760s George lived at North Cave Hall where he started work on a number of ambitious landscaping improvements to the grounds. He promoted a bill for enclosing the open fields of North Cave, which was passed in 1764-5. This included the blocking up of the road which ran to the north of the church and Hall, diverting the Beverley Road to its present route to the south.

Financial difficulties necessitated the sale of his North Cave Estate and in 1773 he sold it for £16,000 to his neighbour Robert Burton of Hotham. George Montgomery Metham died in 1793 and it is believed he retired to Bath where he ended his life in abject poverty.

North Cave Hall was demolished soon after the sale of the estate and in 1863 Sarah Burton of Hotham Hall sold the site to Church Commissioners for an extension to the churchyard. Although part of the wall to the grounds still exists, incorporated as part of the boundary wall that runs from the church to Manor Farm East, there is no trace left of the former medieval manor house.

All Saints' Church

It is believed that there was an unendowed stone built church at North Cave in 1086 when the Domesday book was compiled. Parts of a much earlier building survive in the base of the tower, and the stone, set in the gable above the doorway of the South porch (built in 1753), may be part of the original doorway.

The present church dedicated to All Saints' was built of the local oolitic limestone and consists of a chancel, north and south transepts, nave with south porch and west tower. When the church was dedicated in 1318 it was described as newly built although it had in fact replaced a much older stone building.

Major restoration work to the building was undertaken in 1874, 1892 and again in 1931. In 1974 the roof of the south aisle was renewed and in 1989 further restoration took place. The main churchyard was enlarged in 1866 and again in 1934 when a piece of land opposite the church was donated by a local benefactor. The churchyard was extended for a third time in 1996 when 3 acres of glebe land was consecrated allowing room for a further 140 burial plots.

A former vicar of North Cave, the Reverend Richard Browne was accused of heresy in 1534. It is thought that the offence committed by the vicar may have occurred in Hull as the penance for it was served there.

Although no records have survived stating what the transgression was, it is quite likely that the Reverend Browne had preached a public sermon directed against King Henry VIII who in that year had broken ties with Rome, controversially proclaiming himself as the Head of the Church of England.

King Henry VIII dealt ruthlessly with any opposition, Catholic or Protestant, to his position as supreme head of the Church of England. For example, in that same year several churchmen were hanged for daring to openly speak out against him. A year later in 1535, among even more executions, John Fisher of Beverley who was the Bishop of Rochester was beheaded for refusing to acknowledge the King as the supreme head of the church.

The Reverend Browne was forced to make a public recantation of his crime in Hull, both on Sunday and on market day. Dressed only in his shirt and barefoot he was made to carry a great faggot (bundle of sticks) in his arms around the outside of Holy Trinity Church, Hull. The faggot represented the wood to be used at the burning of a heretic (a disbeliever in the accepted religion). Fortunately, due to his public recantation, he was spared this fate.

Holy Trinity Church was also penalised by having the outside of its doors and windows bound up with thorns and briars. The pavement leading to the church was torn up and the bells were taken down, such was the wrath of the King for the Reverend Browne's misdeed.

The clock in All Saints' Church tower was donated in 1851 by George Baron, who had an estate at Drewton. The clock, made by James Harrison of Hull was reconditioned by William Potts & Sons, Clock Restorers of Leeds in 1950 and again by the same company in 1989. Some parts were completely replaced and the clock was altered to run automatically. Money was raised to pay for this work on the clock by the North Cave Parish Council and local villagers.

In October 1989 the Vicar, The Reverend Peter Hayward was astonished to receive a blank white envelope containing an anonymous note and a donation of fifty £20 notes, towards the restoration fund. During the same year a total of £37,000 was expended on repairing the church fabric.

The tower has six bells in the key of G and they are renowned for their fine peal. Five bells were cast in 1772 by George Doulton & Sons (York) and were recast with the addition of a sixth bell in 1919 by John Taylor & Co. of Loughborough, as both a memorial and a thank-offering for victory in the Great War. Above left, this photograph was taken just before the bells were rehung in 1919. An interesting tablet contained within the church was erected in the memory of William Hicks, who died on 15th December 1899 aged 78 years. Mr. Hicks had earned his living as a local shoe and boot maker. For 24 years he was also a parish clerk and the village bell-ringer, a position he held for 62 years. Above top right, an Edwardian view of All Saints' Church.

Above right, bell-ringer Susan Woods seen here in her wedding dress in the bell tower starting the local custom of "leading off" her own wedding peal. Susan married John Christie (pictured to her immediate left), on Saturday, 28th October 1978. From the far left, Frank Tindale, Elizabeth Tindale, John Little, Alison Redford, Helen Fisher and holding the bell-rope, Geoffrey Hardwick, bell-captain. In 1994 a surprise party was given at North Cave vicarage for Geoffrey in recognition of 50 years service as a bell-ringer at the church.

Just after 1.00 a.m. on the morning of the 5th May 1941 a landmine was seen coming over the right-hand side of Church Street. This high explosive bomb, dropped by parachute exploded in the plantation at the back of the church blowing out the East window. Elsie Wiles now in her eighties recalls, "The night before this bomb dropped, my sister Winifred and I were sitting on the Church wall. We were on duty that evening fire-watching for the village. We could see the bombing over Hull and the sky was all lit up with the fires. The sky was a complete blaze of red. The following night the bit of wall where we had been sitting wasn't there any more, having been blown up when the landmine dropped."

On the 1st January 1900, local man Justice T. Blanshard pictured right, took on the post of Verger and Sexton at All Saints' Church and was still in the post 30 years later. Justice lived at No. 15, Nordham and was a jobbing gardener by trade. For over 42 years he was also a bell-ringer at the Church. When Justice died on the 2nd September 1932 aged 78 years he was laid to rest in the churchyard and was buried in his verger's robes.

A vicarage house is first mentioned in 1764 and was built of stone and thatch, and had three living rooms and three bedrooms. Following its demolition the present vicarage was built in 1823 on the same site, south of the church. It was enlarged in 1831 by Canon John Jarratt, vicar from 1830-1890. Canon Jarratt was a member of a land owning family which developed Kingston Square and the adjacent Jarratt Street in Hull. One of their streets built on John Jarratt's land on Beverley Road, was named Cave Street, in recognition of his rural parish. The north wing of the vicarage was demolished c.1950.

In 1832 Henry Burton of Hotham founded a new Church of England Girls' School in Church Street (pictured right), which was extended in 1870. In 1903 the administration of both the boys' school in Westgate and the girls' school was taken over by the East Riding County Council and in 1934 both schools were combined with all pupils being taught in the girls' school. A new co-educational primary school was opened in Station Road in 1974 and the old school building is now a private dwelling.

Above, celebrating Queen Victoria's Diamond Jubilee in 1897. These schoolgirls are holding their patriotic sashes which they had made from red, white and blue material.

Taken c.1930 this photograph shows some of the younger pupils dancing round the Maypole, which was kept in the schoolyard.

Right, from the left, Miss Mason, Miss Newmarch and Miss Foster and seated Miss Moles, the Headmistress. Miss Grace Irene Newmarch, later became Mrs. Falkner. Grace died in 1986 at the age of 96 years and in her will she left a substantial sum of money to All Saints' Church. An amount of money is provided from that bequest to annually purchase sweets for the village schoolchildren. The sweets are handed out on or about the date of her birthday, the 7th March.

Below, a class of pupils photographed in the schoolyard c.1950.

The Village Playing Field is situated opposite the old girls' school. The field was once a titheyard which abutted upon a thatched stone tithe barn which stood in the vicarage grounds until the early 19th century. Here, tithes amounting to a tenth of the annual produce of land or labour were taken as a tax for the support of the Church and its clergy. During the 1960s a Playing Fields Committee was formed to raise money to purchase the field. In 1971 Mrs. L. F. Judge formally opened it as the Village Playing Field. In recent years a children's adventure playground has been added. In 1983 a £20,000 brick pavilion was built to replace the old wooden pavilion. The new building serves four cricket teams and two football squads besides other social activities.

At one time there were three mills in North Cave which were all in working use into the 20th century. All three mills were situated on the North Cave Beck which runs through the village. Mires Beck and Drewton Beck from Weedley Springs join together near Manor Farm East to form the North Cave Beck.

Pictured right, the Upper Mill, situated to the west of the Paper Mill has a datestone above the old doorway, inscribed with the year 1730, and which is likely to be from the original building.

In the mid 19th century it was known as High Mill, although it is now known locally as Frankish's Mill after the last miller Aaron Frankish, who ceased milling in 1945. The old millstones have been incorporated into the entrance which is now a dwelling.

Further down on North Cave Beck was Low Mill. The mill has long since been demolished, but the mill-house is still occupied.

The Primitive Methodist Chapel

On the right of Quaker Lane (a cart track leading to the old Paper Mill from Church Street), was the former site of the earliest Primitive Methodist Chapel in Yorkshire.

William Clowes the co-founder of the Primitive Methodist movement, a breakaway faction of the Wesleyan Methodists came to the area to preach in 1819. He gained a strong following in Elloughton, Brantingham, Ellerker, South Cave, North Cave and North Newbald and societies were quickly established in those villages.

Clowes, accompanied by another great evangelist 'Praying Johnny' Oxtoby of Warter, visited North Cave on Sunday, 28th February 1819 and he later commented in his journal, "At North Cave there was a little disorder, arising from some persecutors throwing water through the air-holes of the barn upon the people; but notwithstanding this the presence of God was powerfully felt ..."

Local man Richard William Simpson, a shoemaker, hearing Clowes preach invited him to tea and promised to build at his own expense a chapel, which he would let at a small rent to the society.

True to his word, Mr. Simpson showed William Clowes and Johnny Oxtoby a plot of land which he owned in North Cave upon which he offered to build them a chapel. Seeing the land situated on the corner of Quaker Lane, near to Church

Above, the old Primitive Methodist Chapel was converted into a warehouse but later fell into disrepair and was finally demolished about 1920.

Street, Johnny Oxtoby was overjoyed and clapping his hands he exclaimed, "Praise the Lord, this is the place where the Lord intends his ark to rest." The chapel was opened by Mr. and Mrs. John Harrison and Mr. John Woolhouse on the 20th July 1819 and remained in constant use until a new larger Primitive Chapel was erected in Westgate in 1870. Following the demolition of the original Primitive Methodist Chapel, its datestone of 1819 was saved and it is now in the possession of the chapel in Westgate.

The Society of Friends

The Society of Friends was founded in 1647 by George Fox. This Protestant Christian sect challenged the authority of the Church of England by praying in their own way, refusing to take oaths, to bear arms and to pay religious tithes.

As a consequence, members of the Society of Friends were frequently persecuted and prosecuted by law for failing to conform to the established church. Followers of the movement became known as "Quakers," a name given to them by Judge Bennett at Derby because Fox bade him and those present to *"Quake at the Word of the Lord."*

Despite the persecution and suffering the movement survived. George Fox was a frequent visitor to the East Riding in the mid 17th century where he had a considerable following. Meetings of the Society of Friends were held at North Ferriby, Elloughton, Brantingham, North Cave and Hotham.

Before the Act of Toleration in 1689, which allowed for more religious toleration towards nonconformists, meetings were illegal and those found taking part in them were frequently taken before the local magistrates and imprisoned or heavily fined.

It is on record that, *" A meeting was held at the house of Elizabeth Padley of North Cave to which Thomas Forge, priest of that town, came with officers and watchmen and took the names of several persons in order to prosecute them."* As a result, Samuel Padley was fined the sum of £20.10s.0d. for attendance and Jonas Booth was fined £10.0s.0d. for praying at a meeting.

Thomas Forge, the vicar of North Cave was one of the most zealous in the persecution of Quakers operating within his parish during the 17th century. Records of the North Cave Monthly Meetings, now in the custody of the Hull Society of Friends, contain numerous accounts of money sent to various members while in prison and for the relief of their families.

Meeting Houses were later built at Elloughton and North Cave and both had burial grounds, although by the 1740s it was North Cave that had become the centre for the monthly meetings for the area. Membership drastically declined during the mid 19th century. The North Cave Meeting House was closed in 1865 and by 1888 it had been demolished.

A new property was built on the site in 1892 incorporating some of the old stones and it became known as 'Quaker Cottage' (14, Church Street). A former burial ground belonging to the Quakers now lies under the garage, drive, and a small lawn of the property and all that remains are a few scattered gravestones.

A nearby well, situated behind Quaker Cottage, was originally dedicated to St. Helen and has for many years been known as Quaker's Well. At one time the circular stone well was built up above ground level with bricks and covered with a corrugated iron roof.

Very little of the stonework is now left, but it was in constant domestic use up to 1937 as a main source of drinking water. Jack Blacker remembers that as a child it was his job to fetch a couple of buckets of water from the well before and after school until 1950 when piped water was brought into the village from North Newbald.

In March 1998 a grisly discovery was made by workmen digging the foundations for two new houses in Church Street. Work was halted after a shallow grave containing fifteen skeletons was unearthed. Archaeologists were of the opinion that the remains dated from the late 17th or early 18th century and were probably members of a Nonconformist sect.

In May 1998, the remains were reburied in the Quaker burial plot in Spring Bank cemetery in Hull, although it is by no means certain the remains were members of the former Quaker sect in North Cave.

Still visible in the garden of Quaker Cottage are these old Quaker gravestones. The stone on the right is typical showing only the initials and the date of death. The stone on the left dated 1866 was one of the last of the burials on the site and has more details.

The Reverend Christopher Nesse, M.A. was a Puritan and typical of those who were persecuted for refusing to conform to certain Catholic practices contained within the Book of Common Prayer. Born at North Cave in 1621, he was educated at a private school in South Cave from whence he went to St. John's College, Cambridge. After graduating, he preached for a time at South Cliffe Chapel under the supervision of his uncle, Reverend William Brearcliffe, Vicar of North Cave. An Act of Uniformity in May 1662 demanded that ministers pledge that they would consent to everything contained within the Book of Common Prayer or lose their living. The object of the Act was to expunge the Puritans, comprising the Quakers, Presbyterians, Baptists and Congregationalists. No less than two thousand ministers nationwide and including Reverend Nesse voluntarily forsook their churches, their parsonages and their livings. Excommunicated four times, he removed to London in 1675 where he preached to a private congregation in Fleet Street. He died there in 1705, aged 84 years and was buried in the famous Nonconformist burial ground of Bunhill Fields, having served 60 years in the Ministry.

Taken sometime in the 1890s this photograph shows workers in the process of preparing to hoop wheels. From left to right, Frank Pickering, (blacksmith); Mr. Hicks, Snr; Tom Henry Hicks, William Stattersly, (moulder); Bob Saunders (with wheel) and Mr. William Neale. The original blacksmith and joinery workshops that had fronted Church Street were demolished and a house built on the site for the Hicks family. New workshops were built on the site of these open sheds seen in the background of this photograph. Earlier in the 19th century, the business had been run by the Saunders family. It was here that the Saunders family developed a popular light wooden plough which became known in agricultural circles as the "North Cave Plough". In the early 1890s the foundry was operated by Saunders & Hicks and then in 1897 by Tom Henry Hicks, who manufactured and repaired iron and wooden ploughs and other agricultural implements and machinery. Tom was the son of William Hicks, shoemaker of Nordham and had served his apprenticeship as a joiner and wheelwright at James Pearson's workshop in Hotham. Some of the foundry's other regular customers included the Newport brickyards and local builders' merchants who were supplied with household fire-grates, roadside gully grates and drainage castings. Tom's three sons Harry and Charles and later Tom Jnr, followed their father into the business which by 1929 had become T. H. Hicks & Sons. Harry worked as a wheelwright and Charles worked in the foundry. Harry died in 1936. Following Tom Snr's death in the early 1950s Charles left the business which was taken over by his youngest brother Tom Edward. The business carried on until 1979 when it was sold and the forge and foundry were subsequently cleared to make way for a large detached house.

Right, this rare photograph, taken inside the foundry by Anthony Jarman in the early 1960s, shows a wooden jib which would not now conform with current fire, health and safety regulations. The furnace itself was an upended old traction engine boiler. The fan to build up the heat was a wooden paddle-type wheel, driven by an electric motor. Prior to this the furnace was powered by a Petters 'Victory Model' paraffin engine.

Above, another view taken in the early 1960s by Anthony Jarman inside the foundry. Ernie Coates is on the left in the photograph with Gordon McDonald and Eric Johnson on the right, tapping a ladle full of the molten metal from the furnace prior to casting.

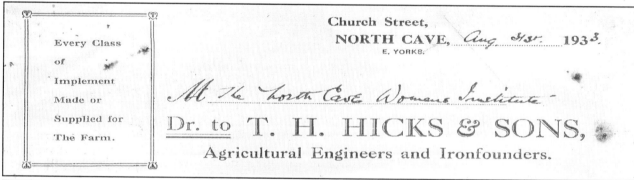

Every Class
of
Implement
Made or
Supplied for
The Farm.

Church Street,
NORTH CAVE, *Aug. 1st,* 193*5.*
E. YORKS.

At the North Cave Womans Institute

Dr. to T. H. HICKS & SONS,
Agricultural Engineers and Ironfounders.

Above, this controversial 85ft high steel chimney attached to the foundry was erected in 1972 to comply with stringent anti-pollution regulations. It loomed prominently over the centre of the village until April 1990 when it was demolished to make way for a detached house.

The Black Swan, (known locally as The Mucky Duck), was in existence in 1787 and was rebuilt in 1813 by Thomas Dean. His two daughters Mary and Caroline were bonnet makers and it is believed that during the 1840s the 'snug', which formed the small single storey section of the building, was used as a shop where the local ladies bought trimmings for dresses and hats. It is said that the inn is haunted and different eye witnesses have reported a middle-aged lady in Victorian dress wandering around the upper part of the building. During the 1960s when Mrs. Jean Brent was landlady, a number of sightings of the ghostly lady took place. On one particular occasion a lodger fled from the bedroom and refused to return to it. Mrs. Brent's son Tony recalls he also

witnessed the lady coming through a wardrobe and walking across the bedroom before disappearing. The wardrobe was situated where there was once a doorway leading from the top of the stairs. The stairs were removed and re-sited elsewhere in the building during renovations to the inn many years before it was occupied by the Brents. Interestingly, a skull was discovered embedded in an out-house wall. The stone had crumbled exposing the skull which is believed to have been that of a baby. The landlady's daughter Hazel took it to school and it was from that time that the apparitions began.

Left, Henry Rispin was a carrier and a fellmonger at No. 37, Church Street. To local villagers he was the "knacker" - a term applied to a man who slaughtered horses or cattle, who dealt with hides and skins and carried out a respectable and useful business. After the hides had been removed he would take the carcases by cart to Newport Road where he had an open site on which was a boiler shed. The bones would be boiled to make glue. Betty Luke recalls the gruesome sights of Henry regularly bringing an uncovered cart load of dead horses into the village. Wilf Lundy who lived in nearby Kiln Row (now demolished), would buy hooves from Henry, clean them out and make pin cushions which he would sell.

Right, Thomas Dudding Newmarch painter and decorator examining the clock face on the tower at All Saints' Church. In the 1850s his great grandfather Francis Ball Newmarch, painter and tallow chandler, lived in what later became known as Denmark House from which he ran a paint and wallpaper shop. In 1860 Francis bought Upper Mill and became miller there. Francis had 16 sons, every one of whom followed in the family trade of painting. In the early 1940s, Douglas Newmarch, only son of Thomas, married and later moved to North Cliffe, finally ending the family's business interests in North Cave.

The little shop (now a grocery store and newsagency), seen here on the left in this photograph taken c.1924 was originally a single storey cottage to which a brick upper storey was added around the turn of the 20th century. For a number of years it was George Harrison's pork butcher shop with its own slaughterhouse at the rear. The white building a little further up on the left-hand side was William Gelder's joinery shop which was later demolished.

Peter Stone, formerly a local miller, opened a fried fish and chip shop in 1937. It was housed in a wooden hut near to the Black Swan public house in Church Street. Peter had a horse called Violet which pulled a cart containing blocks of lard from Gray's butchers shop in Westgate. Following his retirement, his son Stan took over the business and is seen here with his wife Elsie busy frying. There were two ranges, one for frying chips and one for frying fish and both were heated by coal fired burners. After Stan's death in 1967 the shop was managed by his son Malcolm for a short period before it was finally closed and demolished in 1969.

Above, an advertisement dated 1929 for Harry Raymond Moore's Pork Butcher shop formerly at number 69, Church Street.

Above left, Henry Hardwick, P.C. 120 of the East Riding Constabulary was the resident North Cave village policeman between 1908 -1913. He lived in a police house on the corner of Appleton Lane, still locally referred to as Policeman's Lane or Corner. Above right, Arthur John Luke as a young policeman in 1912. During the Second World War former Howden police constable Luke became the War Reserve Policeman for North Cave. He had for some years been the lodge keeper for Hotham Hall following his premature retirement from the police force after sustaining a serious injury in pursuit of a felon. Many inhabitants held P.C. Luke in high regard and recall that he kept up public morale during the war years. He was succeeded by P.C. Ken Foxon who was later replaced by only one police constable based at South Cave.

Sir (William) Alfred Gelder

Born in 1855 at number 30, Church Street, pictured right, William Alfred Gelder (known as Alfred), was the son of William, a joiner and wheelwright. He attended the village school and grew up to become an architect and a prominent civic figure on the City Council of Kingston upon Hull.

He served as Lord Mayor of Hull for a record five years in succession from 1898-1903 and was also a Member of Parliament for the city. In his final year as Lord Mayor he was host to the Prince and Princess of Wales (the future King George V and Queen Mary), when they made an official visit to Hull in 1903. The knighthood which he received shortly afterwards was attributed partly to this occasion.

Sir Alfred, however, is best remembered for his important work as an architect. With his partner Llewellyn Kitchen, he designed some of the City's largest emporiums, flour and oil mills and Methodist churches. This was in addition to the part he played in remodelling the crowded slums and narrow streets of central Hull. Jameson Street, King Edward Street and the one named in his honour, Alfred Gelder Street, were all part of his scheme to create new wide thoroughfares. His last great work for Hull was during the 1930s when Queen's Dock was filled in and Queen's Garden's was laid out in its place.

Following his death at the age of 86 years in 1941, the Labour Lord Mayor of Hull (Councillor Sydney H. Smith), said of him, *"Sir Alfred was beyond doubt the maker of modern Hull, I remember seeing him the day after the May blitz. Much of his life's work had been wiped out and he might have been forgiven if he had felt crushed, but next day he attended a meeting to see what could be done to rehouse some of the traders ..."* Sir Alfred Gelder was laid to rest near the east window in the churchyard of All Saints' Church in his native home of North Cave.

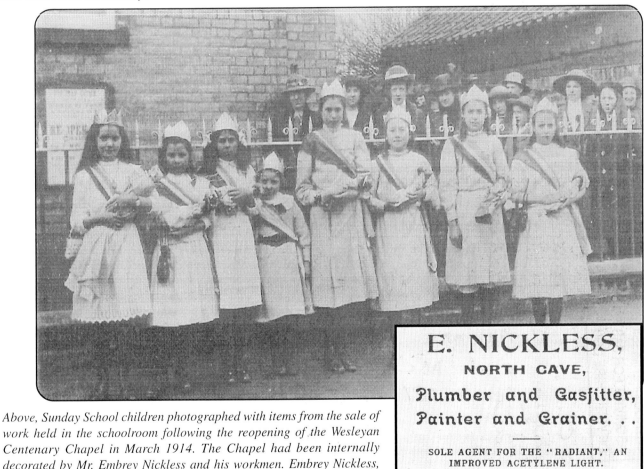

Above, Sunday School children photographed with items from the sale of work held in the schoolroom following the reopening of the Wesleyan Centenary Chapel in March 1914. The Chapel had been internally decorated by Mr. Embrey Nickless and his workmen. Embrey Nickless, lived at No. 23, Church Street and had carried on the family business

started by his father Edward Nickless who was a house painter and plumber. Mr. Charles Pearson performed the ceremony of the reopening of the chapel doors which was followed by a lecture given by the Reverend James Hanby on George Fox, the founder of the Quaker movement and his famous suit of leather. The first Wesleyan Chapel in North Cave was built in 1823 in Westgate, but due to rising membership new premises were needed. In 1839, the centenary of the start of John Wesley's travels, a new chapel was erected in Church Street. A year later the old chapel in Westgate became the Boys' School. The Wesleyan Centenary Chapel flourished until just after the Second World War when membership began falling. By October 1960, the Primitive Methodists and Wesleyans had united becoming a new single Methodist Society worshipping in the former Primitive Chapel in Westgate. The Centenary Chapel in Church Street was closed and the building now functions as a warehouse while the former schoolroom is used as the Newport and District Young Farmers' Club.

Left, the Reverend John Wesley who preached at North Cave on 2nd July 1761. He recorded in his journal of the occasion, "I set out early for North Cave, 20 computed miles from York. I preached there at nine to a deeply serious congregation and was much refreshed."

Above, the former Wesleyan Centenary Chapel in 1999.

The building on the right was originally a garage built for Mr. Anthony Eland Scott who owned the main village shop in Westgate. Miss Eva Parker (inset), later purchased the property which became No. 63, Church Street and converted it into a house. In the late 1920s she had an extension built from where she opened a bakery and confectionery shop. Following her retirement in 1948 her nephew George Evison and his wife Amy purchased the business and continued it as a bakery and grocers until 1958. Stan and Violet Jones were the last owners of the shop selling

children's clothes, wool and groceries. Mr. Alan Hall bought the property in 1988 and over a period of about a year he demolished the old extension which is seen here before demolition work began.

Above, local 'Band of Hope' members taking part in a North Cave Temperance Society Festival in 1909.

The Temperance Hall

The Temperance Hall was built in 1851 by William Hewson, a grocer, draper and sub-postmaster in Westgate. Temperance Societies were introduced into many towns and villages from the 1830s in the hope that they would help to curtail the level of drunkenness among the general populace. Members of the Society were encouraged to abstain from alcohol altogether and sign 'The Pledge'.

The North Cave Temperance Society was formed c.1840. The movement was certainly flourishing with some 129 adults and 40 juveniles as members and at that time it was reported that it, "*Had been the means of rescuing some drunkards ... and had effected much good in the village.*"

An annual tea party was held and on the 19th June 1840 the event took place in a large barn belonging to Mr. Richard Blossom, a local farmer. The Independent Order of the Rechabites, the village friendly society, (founded 1840), led the procession of members on a parade through North Cave to the parish church where the Reverend Terry delivered his sermon advocating the cause of abstinence.

The Temperance Movement was greatly supported by the Wesleyans and the Primitive Methodist Chapel and a 'Band of Hope' allied to the Methodist chapels was flourishing by 1896. In 1901 there were some 40 juvenile and 20 adult members but these numbers gradually decreased and the group was disbanded by 1919. In 1923 the Temperance Hall was bought by Colonel William Henton Carver for a meeting place for the North Cave and Hotham Boy Scouts, who much later merged with the South Cave troop. During the Second World War the hall was used by the Home Guard as their headquarters.

In 1967 it was given to the British Legion. Near to the old Temperance Hall is the small village green where a lime tree was planted in 1897 to celebrate Queen Victoria's Diamond Jubilee. Unfortunately the tree did not survive and a replacement lime tree stands in its place. In 1977 the Parish Council planted some flowering cherry trees on the green and around other parts of the village as part of a nationwide tree planting promotion.

Right, the old Temperance Hall in 1999 standing derelict and empty. Below, local children taking part in the British Legion Annual Fancy Dress competition at the Temperance Hall c.1946.

Waterloo Will

William Howarth was born at Fishlake, near Doncaster in 1789. As a young man he was a soldier in the 33rd Regiment of Foot and fought under the Duke of Wellington at the Battle of Waterloo. He was badly wounded in the fighting and discharged. On returning home he found his widowed mother had died and as a consequence he was homeless.

William commenced a new career as an itinerant ballad singer in 1814 and became known as "Waterloo Will." He married in 1819 and, with his wife Esther, he attended all the principal fairs, markets and races from Berwick upon Tweed, Northumberland to Boston in Lincolnshire.

William Howarth known as "Waterloo Will" was a rag and bone man for many years in North Cave and is pictured in the drawing above with his donkey and cart.

He was a notorious character and prone to violent behaviour after excessive drinking sessions in which he frequently indulged. Being six feet tall and heavily built he was an object of terror to the peace officers who tried to control him. He was brought before the Lord Mayor of York no less than 13 times in one year. On one occasion at Pocklington after having drunk seven half-pints of rum (or 'Ram-a-tam' as he called it), at the Buck Inn, he was refused an eighth, which he had already paid for and was turned out onto the street.

Highly exasperated at his ejection he was so disruptive that it took three constables to restrain him and put him in irons. He was taken to the local unattended village lock-up from which he managed to escape by breaking a hole in the wall.

Whilst he was engaged in making the hole through which to escape a bystander said, *"Waterloo, you have got the hole large enough now; you can get through."* But his reply was, *"No, I walked straight through and I'll walk straight out,"* and he continued to batter the wall until he could walk out.

In 1838 at the age of 49 years he settled in North Cave with his wife and they had two children, Thomas and Esther. However, he still occasionally went on singing excursions around the country. As well as working as a straw carrier for local farmers during threshing times, he started a rag and bone business. He had two dogs broken into harness so that they could pull a small cart round the neighbourhood with an assorted cargo, consisting of nuts, oranges and various items of fruit.

On one occasion whilst on his usual rounds he called at the Black Swan for a drop of 'Ram-a-tam,' and whilst he was drinking, the dogs attacked a cat which had suddenly appeared. Unfortunately, in the commotion, the dogs and cart collided with a lady passer-by, ending up with William's goods scattered all over the road and the lady in the cart. Shortly afterwards he managed to obtain a donkey to pull the cart instead of a dog.

His wife Esther became a methodist and regularly attended the local chapel becoming determined to change William's way of life. She refused to attend any more fairs and races with him and with the help of the local chapel raised a subscription, to purchase the whole of William's stock of ballads.

The ballads were then ceremoniously burnt by his wife and members of the chapel on the Howarth's coal fire. Nevertheless, despite his wife's protestations he carried on singing and drinking for a number of years.

On the 26th December 1846, heavily intoxicated he had taken shelter in some stables at Newport during a severe snowstorm and almost froze to death. He eventually reached his home but in a wretched condition.

Shortly afterwards Mr. J. Pearson, Mr. Stather and Mr. J. Crosby three members of the North Cave Temperance Society called upon him and implored him for the sake of his wife and family to sign *"The Pledge."* He agreed and from that day until the time of his death he remained an abstainer from alcoholic drinks.

William became a regular worshipper at the chapel and was appointed the "Village Bellman." He also assisted at Temperance Meetings in the district, telling his story of how he had been saved from the "evils of drink." William would often repeat this little ditty he had made up to explain how his life had changed since he had rejected alcohol,

> *"Who lives there? - who do you think?*
> *An old drunken soldier, who used to like drink;*
> *But now he's teetotal and keeps out of debt,*
> *He lives in a neat little cottage,*
> *With its back t'd beck."*

In 1866 at the age of 77 years William died and was buried in the west end of North Cave churchyard. Shortly before he died he expressed a wish that, if ever an epitaph was to be placed on his tombstone, the following should be written,

> *"Under this hill lies Waterloo Will,*
> *Who lived and died a venture,*
> *A plague to his wife all the days of his life,*
> *And to the farmer a daily tormenter.*
> *Cross he lived and cross he died:*
> *Quietly buried and nobody cried.*
> *Where he is, and how he fares,*
> *Nobody knows and nobody cares."*

William had become a much reformed character in his later years after signing *"The Pledge."* His funeral was extremely well attended and Canon John Jarratt, the Vicar of All Saints' Church, North Cave officiated at the service. Despite his request, however, no gravestone was ever erected to his memory.

Nordham

Since the early 18th century the northernmost road and area of the village has been known as Nordham (earlier spelt as 'Nordum'). It is connected to the rest of the village by Church Lane and further west, by Palmer Lane later known as Blossom Lane which crosses the beck by Froscoles Bridge.

Before enclosure in 1765 the original road to Beverley led from Nordham which ran parallel with Church Street, due east and north of All Saints' Church. However, after enclosure, the Nordham road was severed at the point where Hotham Lodge now stands and diverted to its present route southwards into Church Lane to join up with Church Street. This street in turn was extended eastwards to re-establish the link with Beverley Road.

A view of Nordham taken c.1905.

Below, Manor Farm West built in the early 18th century has long since ceased to function as a farm. The old farmhouse is now a private dwelling. During the 1830s it was farmed by Richard Blossom the brother of Thomas Blossom, who was a missionary in Tahiti and Eimo in Polynesia from 1820-1843. Following his retirement as a missionary, Thomas returned to live in Westgate, North Cave at the home of Matthew Tindale a tax collector. Thomas became his assistant and was still in this occupation in 1851 at the age of 73 years. He was also a regular member of the Congregationalist Church situated in the West End of South Cave until his death at the age of 77 years, on 5th February 1855. He was buried in the west end of the churchyard of All Saints' Church, North Cave, where his tombstone can still be clearly seen near the entrance to the church doorway. Richard's son Thomas took over from his father and was still farming at Manor Farm West in 1892, with his wife Ann and seven children. Nearby Palmer Lane became known as Blossom Lane sometime in the early 19th century, taking its name from this well-known North Cave family.

Thomas Blossom

Mr. and Mrs. George Foster came to live at Manor Farm West in 1954. At that time George farmed some 125 acres which over the years was gradually reduced with the sale of various parcels of land. Following George's retirement in 1991 the rest of the land and livestock was sold but the farmhouse pictured right, was retained as a private residence.

Left, George Foster on his Ferguson tractor at the rear of Manor Farm West in 1954. On the left in the photograph can be seen the old stone dairy shed now demolished

Right, Mrs. Nancy Foster in 1954 with her shire-horse known as Dolly.

Above, an Edwardian view looking along the footpath from Church Street towards Nordham. The old Paper Mill can be seen in the foreground and was in use as a corn mill until 1925. Stan Stone is recorded as being the last miller there. The mill and cottages were converted into a single modern dwelling in 1976. Its name originated in the early 18th century when, for some time coarse paper was made there. Local man Ernie Coates who worked for the Hicks Foundry in Church Street for many years recalls that shortly after he started work there in 1948, all the machinery from the Paper Mill, which was mainly made of cast iron, was removed by Hicks and melted down for scrap metal.

Belgrave Square

In 1936 a pair of semi-detached houses were built by the council on the former site of Belgrave Square. The square had consisted of ten stone cottages, three of which stood at the front, three at one side and four along the back.

The three cottages at the front of the square were the last to be demolished, the other seven having gone during the 1920s. Mary Hodgson recalls that at different times her family had occupied two of the front properties.

One of these properties had the luxury of four rooms comprising two bedrooms, a kitchen and a front parlour. The remaining nine cottages consisted of one room upstairs and one downstairs. Each cottage had an outside privy which was situated across the road.

All the families shared a communal water pump which had originally stood outside the back kitchen door of one of the front cottages. The pump was used until 1938 when the village got its first supply of piped water and it can still be seen

Belgrave Square c.1922 showing the Hodgson family, Mary with husband Fred, daughters Grace, Mary and Betty, their son, Fred and Pussyfoot the cat.

standing in what is now the front garden of number 46, Nordham. Despite the cramped living conditions Mary recalls that a Mr. Rueben Whiteman and his wife Emma brought up their six children in one of the smaller cottages in the square.

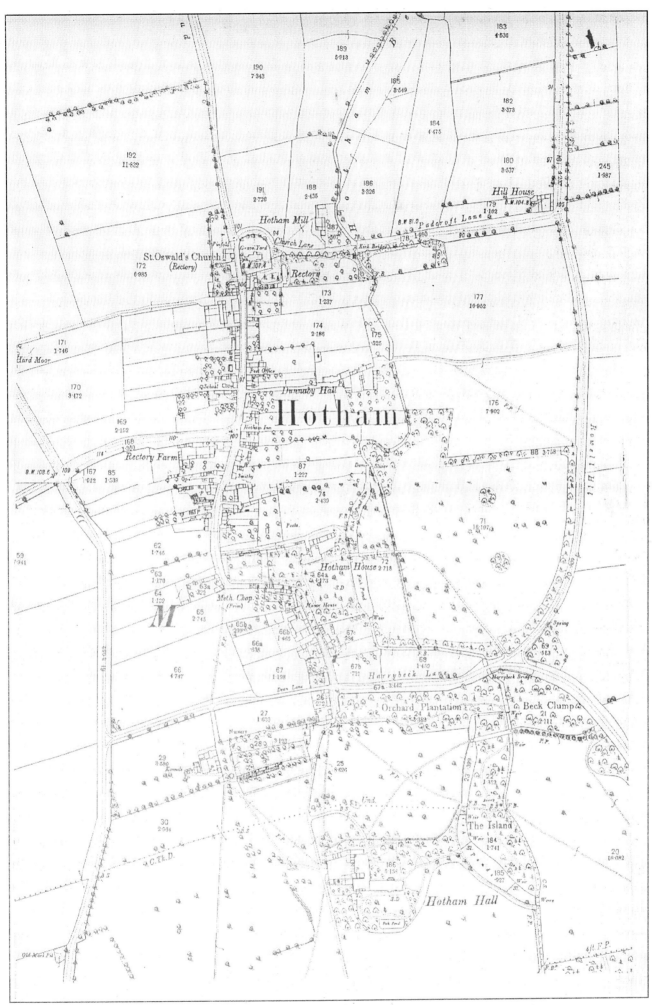

Map of Hotham 1890

The Development of Hotham

The village of Hotham lies about one mile north-east of North Cave and is believed to have developed from an Anglo-Saxon settlement. Its name which means 'shelter' is of Scandinavian origin and was probably derived from the fact that the village lies in a shallow valley.

An Anglo-Saxon site was discovered during the early 1990s on the border of the parish boundary which points to it having been an important market area. A number of coins and associated metalwork covering the 8th and 9th centuries were recovered from the site and recorded by archaeologists.

Like many other villages in the area there are signs of human habitation well before the Anglo-Saxons arrived. A hoard consisting of at least nine palstave Axes and one palstave mould dating from the Bronze Age was discovered in 1867 during ploughing on Hotham Carrs. Unfortunately, the greater portion of this hoard was sold to a rag and bone dealer and subsequently to a brass founder in Hull who melted them down.

Substantial remains of a logboat thought to date from the Iron Age (c.300 BC), were discovered during the mid 1960s by a firm of drainage contractors near South Carr Farm, Walling Fen, situated on the outskirts of the village. The logboat was taken out of the ground and despite its good condition it was abandoned in a nearby pond and left to rot.

Larger than the Hasholme logboat, found c.1977 about 2 miles from this site (near Holme on Spalding Moor) and with many similar features, the South Carr Farm logboat gives a further indication of the use of the Humber estuarine inlet and its associated watercourses during the later prehistoric period.

Archaeological finds have revealed the presence of a substantial Iron Age industry on the margins of the former creek system. It is thought quite possible that both logboats were associated with this. The Hasholme logboat is now on public display at the Hull and East Riding Museum, High Street, Hull.

The Domesday Survey of 1086 records that prior to the Norman Conquest, the subdivided manors of Hotham in Howdenshire were held by noblemen, Turchill, Orme, Basin, Ingrede, Grim and the Bishop of Durham. Following the Norman Conquest in 1066, there were already over 650 acres of cultivated land in Hotham and about 100 people lived and worked in the village.

In 1069, a year after King William I's victorious armies moved northwards, the population, together with other communities from the East Riding revolted against the Normans and revenge was sought.

King William kept the manors which he wanted in the East Riding which included Market Weighton, Warter, Driffield, Pocklington, Bridlington and Burton Agnes. The Norman army laid waste the remaining manors, wilfully destroying buildings, burning crops and killing indiscriminately. Many fled south to the prosperous Midlands whilst the outcome for the remaining population was starvation, poverty and slavery. The East Riding did not fully recover until well into the 12th century.

During this period of strife Hotham's population had been reduced to forty people. There were fifteen derelict cottages and nearly all the land laid waste. It was not until the mid 13th century that the population recovered to its pre-Norman level.

Sir John de Trehouse, Lord of Kilkenny of Ireland who had fought with William the Conqueror at the Battle of Hastings, was rewarded with a castle and lands in Northamptonshire and

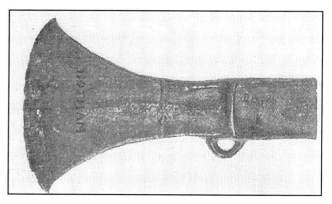

In 1884 a single palstave axe was found close to where a hoard of similar axes and their mould had been discovered in 1867. This axe and the mould are now in the possession of the Hull and East Riding Museum, High Street, Hull.

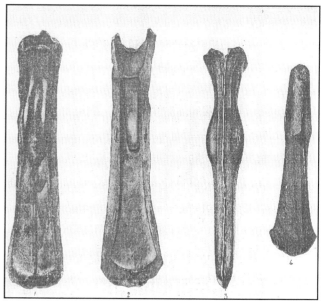

Above, a detailed view of the mould used for casting bronze axes of the palstave type, which was found with the hoard of axes, nearly all of which were damaged and broken and seemed to have been gathered together for the purpose of being re-cast. Although a number of stone moulds have been found elsewhere, the discovery of bronze moulds such as this one are generally rare. The two sections fit together exactly, which shows that a high degree of skill in bronze casting was attained by these early Britons.

also a grant of the Manor of Hotham. One of his descendents, Peter de Trehouse adopted the name of Hotham.

Although the Hotham family undoubtedly assumed their name from the village, their estate was only a small one. For over 300 hundred years the seat of the Hotham family has been a few miles away at South Dalton, near Beverley. Sir John Hotham, the Governor of Kingston upon Hull is best remembered as having closed the gates on King Charles I in 1642 and was subsequently beheaded as a traitor.

Following the Norman Conquest, Hotham was still made up of a number of subdivided manors, some of which were still held by religious houses which included the Bishop of Durham. The Knights Templars also had an estate here during the 12th century.

The largest manor of Hotham, which included much of North Cave eventually passed into the hands of the Metham family who also had a large estate at Metham, near Howden. The manor was sold in 1773 by George Montgomery Metham who was in financial difficulties and much of it was bought by the Burton family of Hotham Hall.

The present day village of Hotham consists of several old farmhouses in the Main Street and a number of properties which were built in the 18th or 19th century. There are examples of earlier houses built of the local limestone that still survive, the most notable examples being numbers 27 and 30, Main Street. Number 27 is also known as Moss Cottage and is a Grade II listed building which is believed to date to c.1650, although over the centuries it has been renovated and extended.

Following the enclosure of Hotham's fields and commons in 1768 a number of farmhouses were built away from the village. North and South Carr Houses (later North and South Farms) and Snake Hall were all built by 1820. Hill House and Hard Moor situated above the escarpment had also been built by this date. Another outlying house built before 1850 was Rectory Cottage, later named Glebe Farm situated in the Carrs. This area is a low flat tract of ground, formerly marsh, lying on the western border of the parish, adjoining Wallingfen. On the higher ground are situated Moor Farm, later called Hotham Field Farm and Hotham Grange.

Hotham's economic survival had for many centuries been dependant mainly on farming, although during the 18th and 19th centuries much employment was provided either within nearby Hotham Hall or on its estate. During the mid 19th century there were 430 people living in the village and most of the working population were employed by the estate. Other occupations at this time included nine farmers, two shopkeepers, a cheese dealer, farrier, two wheelwrights, a miller, carrier, three boot and shoemakers, a beerhouse owner, blacksmith and a watch and clockmaker.

The village has changed considerably since the Second World War. With the increasing use of motorised transport, large supermarkets and employment opportunities elsewhere, the local population no longer needs a self-supporting community. All the shops and most of the old trades have disappeared. Villagers are no longer reliant mainly on farming or the Hotham Hall Estate for their living. Due to the changing methods of farming, especially the increased mechanisation, there are now only four working farms in the village and a number of former farm buildings have been sold and converted into residential properties. Since the Humberside Structure Plan implemented during the early 1980s, Hotham is classed as a non-selected settlement and housing is limited to infilling between existing properties. This has certainly helped the village to retain its rural characteristics.

A view of the north facing elevation of Hotham Hall.

Ꝺotham Ꝺall

Hotham Hall, a Grade II listed brick and stone building is situated in the parish of North Cave and was built by William Burton the younger in 1719, following the purchase of the estate from a William Robinson.

The Hall and estate descended to Robert Burton who, in 1773 bought the North Cave Manor from his neighbour in North Cave Hall, George Montgomery Metham for £16,000. Robert carried out a number of improvements at the Hall which included rebuilding the stable block to incorporate a central carriage archway. He also added two new wings to the house. Robert died in 1802 and the estate was bequeathed to the grandson of a cousin, Robert Christie Burton.

Robert Christie Burton never married and following his death in 1822, his sister Sarah inherited the estate. Sarah Burton married a General John Clitherow in 1809 but they were divorced in 1819. She was married for a second time to Henry Peters, who took the additional surname of Burton about 1827.

During the Burton family's residency at Hotham Hall, North Cave Hall was demolished and the grounds were merged with those of Hotham Hall. A datestone inscribed "GMM 1683" was removed from North Cave Hall and reset into the pediment of the stables, when Robert was re-building the stable block.

After Sarah's death in 1869 the estate passed to Colonel Edward John Stracey-Clitherow, the cousin of John Christie Clitherow (Sarah's son, who had died in 1865). Stracey had assumed the name Clitherow by Royal Licence in 1865.

Colonel Edward J. Stracey-Clitherow made significant alterations to Hotham Hall including the demolition of the 18th century west wing, replacing it with a new brick wing for use as servants quarters. A large off-centre bow window was added to the south elevation and the large glazed porch to the north elevation later in the 19th century.

In 1900 Edward was succeeded by his brother the Reverend William James Stracey, who also assumed the additional name of Clitherow upon inheriting the estate. He lived at Boston House, Brentford, near London. His son Colonel John Bourchier Stracey-Clitherow (1853-1931), lived at Hotham Hall and there entertained King Edward VII to lunch in 1905.

In 1912 on the death of his father William, John B. Stracey-Clitherow inherited Hotham Hall and the family home of Boston House, in Brentford, London.

In 1897 John B. Stracey-Clitherow married Alice Gurney who was a divorcee. Her son Thomas Claud Gurney from her previous marriage changed his name to Clitherow on inheriting the estate following the death of his stepfather in 1931.

Colonel Thomas Claud Gurney Clitherow died in 1963 and the estate then descended to his daughter Juliet, the wife of John Henton Carver, who died in 1969 and then to their son, Peter Carver. Mrs. Jan Odey, nee Carver, sister to Peter lived in the Hall from 1966 until 1984 when it was sold to Stephen Martin, the managing director of Hull based Arco Ltd.

Colonel E. J. Stracey-Clitherow and his nephew J. B. Stracey-Clitherow were both involved in amassing a large collection of coaching memorabilia. This coach seen here entering the stable yard at Hotham Hall was purchased by them from a Mr. Chandos Pole. It was believed to have been the only survivor of the mail coaches employed on the London-Devonport run. The fastest, known as 'Quicksilver' was the most famous of the fleet and the only Royal Mail coach to bear a name. A keen horseman, J. B. Stracey-Clitherow could often be seen out driving a four-in-hand until a few years before his death in 1931 at the age of 78 years.

On Wednesday, 13th October 1926, the year of the General Strike, Edward Prince of Wales paid a two day visit to Hull. His first official visit was to the HQ of the British Legion (Hull Branch). The Prince then left for Hotham where he stayed overnight as a guest of Colonel John B. Stracey-Clitherow. Hundreds of people congregated in Hotham Park to welcome the Prince who inspected the North Cave Branch of the British Legion. He then inspected the North Cave and Hotham Troop of Boy Scouts, the North Cave Girl Guides and the North Cave and Hotham Brownies. During the proceedings the South Cave Subscription Silver Band, under their conductor Mr. Fred Moore, played a selection of music. The following morning at 7 a.m. the Prince rode out with the Holderness Hunt which had been invited to Hotham Hall for the occasion. As the Prince left the courtyard of Hotham Hall he raised his hat to the crowd and proceeded along the drive to join the huntsmen and dogs into the coombs. He left at 10.00 a.m. to fulfil his first engagement of the day at the National Radiator Company Factory on National Avenue, Hull. This photograph was taken just in front of the Hall. From left to right, Tom Gurney (later Clitherow), H.R.H. Prince of Wales, (who ten years later was to abdicate the throne in favour of marrying an American divorcee, Mrs. Wallis Simpson), Juliet Gurney, (standing), Ann Gurney, (standing), Alice Gurney (far right, standing).

The North Cave Cricket Club was formed in the late 19th century. Its original ground together with a pavilion was situated at Fairfield, on Station Road, North Cave. At the invitation of Colonel J. B. Stracey-Clitherow, a keen sportsman, the club moved to a new site within Hotham Park and only a short distance from Hotham Hall. This photograph, taken in 1914 shows the cricket team with part of the Hall just visible in the background. Following the Colonel's death in 1931 the cricket pitch and pavilion were moved to the other side of the park. Later, they moved to Newport Road and in 1983 moved to their present site at the playing fields in Church Street, North Cave.

Left, members of the Hotham Cricket Club which was formed during the 1950s. The cricket ground was situated in a field belonging to Mr. Bill Lawson of Church Farm, who was at the time the Captain of the North Cave Cricket Club. Lack of support, however, resulted in its demise by the early 1960s.

TO YPRES
347 Miles
IN DEFENDING
THE SALIENT
OUR CASUALTIES
— WERE —
90,000 KILLED.
71,000 MISSING.
410,000 WOUNDED.

Right, this board was originally fixed to a wall adjoining North Cave Lodge. It records the distance to Ypres, 347 miles. In later years the board was removed and placed on the Lodge wall where it can still be seen today. It was placed there by Colonel Tom Claud Gurney Clitherow of Hotham Hall and commemorates the appalling casualties sustained in defending the Salient at Ypres, a Belgian town in West Flanders. During the 1914-18 war the Salient was one of the most fiercely fought battle fronts and it was there that chemical warfare, such as chlorine and mustard gas was introduced and used by both sides. The German machine gun also made its first appearance at this time causing British soldiers to be mown down in their thousands. The third battle of Ypres (also known as Paschendale), July-November 1917 was a long battle fought for the most part in driving rain on already waterlogged ground. This particular battle stands out as an enormous waste of life in that it achieved an advance of only 5 miles of terrority. Moreover, it was of no strategic significance and the allies lost more than 300,000 men. Appalled at the sheer slaughter, it was Colonel Tom Clitherow's intention to remind anyone seeing the board, that Ypres, although on foreign soil was, at 347 miles, really not so far removed from the rural tranquility of North Cave and Hotham.

Around Hotham Village

This photograph taken at the turn of the century shows the North Cave Lodge, at the entrance to Hotham Hall Park. It was built sometime during the 1880s of grey brick and stone.

Below, Number 42, Main Street seen here on the far left in this photograph was the former home of the Withell family. Following the Second World War it became the village post office until 1994. Mrs. Yates was the last post mistress before it closed. In the foreground cows are seen going into Manor Farm.

Above, Mrs. Elizabeth Withall, who was a well-known character in Hotham. During the 1860s she was a land surveyor but later traded as a gun repairer. Towards the end of her life she became a watchmaker. Her husband Thomas had been the village schoolmaster as well as a clock and watchmaker. Several beautifully made examples of his work still exist in houses around the district.

Right, Hotham House built in 1740 stands at the southern end of the village in walled grounds. The lane that runs by the house and now forms part of Main Street was known from 1852 as Amen Lane. In 1772, Sir George Montgomery Metham sold the house and about 30 acres of land to the Reverend Richard Gee. After the death of Richard's widow Hannah in 1826 the estate passed to Gertrude Gee and her husband the Reverend James White. Reverend White was responsible for the design and lay out of the grounds, which include a lake close to the house and a small park extending beyond the beck. In

1868, Reverend White sold the house and estate to Mr. Walter Frances Wrangham. Mr. Robert Henry Micks was the owner of Hotham House from c.1900-33. Above, a photograph taken on Saturday, 11th September 1909 outside Hotham House on the occasion of the marriage of Mr. Micks niece. Subsequently, the property changed hands several times before being sold in 1978 to Mr. M. S. Healey. Alterations and additions to Hotham House at various dates in the late 19th century included extensive remodelling of the interior and refacing of the south frontage to incorporate various extensions.

Below, Mr. Robert H. Micks' garden and domestic staff at Hotham House c.1910. From left to right, Mr. Walker, Joe Lockwood, Gertie Copeland, Mr. Leake, Bert Gray (Head Gardener), Lily Stather, Mr. Drewery (Coachman), Wilf Danby (Under Gardener), Mrs. Underwood, Mrs. Sargenson, Mrs. Lockwood and Mrs. Messenger. From 1949 Mrs. Nellie Grisewood was employed by Mr. and Mrs. Ellison as a domestic servant at Hotham House. Two years later Mr. and Mrs. Upton became the new owners of the property. They employed Nellie for a further 23 years as a domestic help. The progressive introduction of new and improved household appliances and machines consequently reduced the number of domestic staff previously employed. Nellie, however, was deemed indispensable and she worked for six hours each day, five days a week covering a wide range of duties from scrubbing floors, setting fires, cooking and serving guests at dinner-parties. Nellie now aged 86 years still lives in the village in well earned retirement.

Nellie Grisewood

This photograph was taken on Saturday, 13th August 1910 in the grounds of Hotham House and shows members of the Girls' Friendly Society. The Society was founded by the two daughters of James Wilson Tomlinson of Manor Farm, Hotham. Girls would be invited to use the grounds or play tennis at Hotham House. It is not known for how long the Girls' Friendly Society existed but it is remembered that only daughters of local farmers were usually accepted for membership. Village girls from less affluent families were not encouraged to join.

Looking south along Main Street (formerly known as Amen Lane), towards Hotham Hall. This rustic looking building (thought to have been built in the 18th century), on the right in this view was listed as Mrs. Burton's school for girls in 1822.

Right, the only nonconformist chapel in the village was the Primitive Methodist Chapel erected in 1869 on land given by the Wilson family. The Methodist Chapel enjoyed a flourishing membership up until c.1980. The congregation however, had dwindled to only four members by 1989. Two of the remaining members were Connie and Bill Lawson. Bill was the assistant organist for many years. In the same year, following the discovery of a number of serious structural faults in the building, the chapel was finally closed. Shortly afterwards it was sold at auction in the White Hart public house in Westgate, North Cave. Owing to the condition of the chapel's foundations, the new owners demolished the property and rebuilt it in the same style but as a dwelling house, using the same bricks.

Left, during the 1890s Benny Wilson had a small shop built adjoining his house next to the chapel. He took on the position of sub-postmaster, sold groceries and ran a tailoring business from the premises. Older villagers remember that he would deliver post around Hotham on a tricycle. A devout Methodist, Mr. Benny, as he was known locally, was also a preacher and a Sunday School teacher. Following his death in the early 1920s his wife Mary Ann took over the grocery shop until c.1933 when she sold it to Miss Phoebe Parkin. Mr. and Mrs. Matthews were the next owners from c.1938 until their retirement in the early 1980s.

The Hotham Arms has existed since at least 1846. There were two other public houses recorded in the village during the 18th century but only the name of one of them is known. The 'Fox', owned by Hull Brewery was formerly situated at what is now No. 38, Main Street. The Hotham Arms was first known as the Queen's Arms, and secondly as the Hotham Inn, but by 1930 it was known by its present name. This view taken c.1910 shows a large elm tree which stood opposite the inn before it was cut down in 1920 in order to provide a suitable site on which to erect the village war memorial. The Hotham Arms is reputed to be haunted by the ghost of former landlord Fred Sargeson who died on the premises in the mid 1950s. Mr. Chris Harris, landlord of the pub in 1980 reported the sound of ghostly footsteps, doors opening by themselves and the apparition of Mr. Sargeson visiting an outhouse at 7.30 one morning. On investigation, the ghostly form disappeared. Many local inhabitants remain very sceptical and believe the story to be more imagined than factual.

Above, this photograph was taken in 1923 shortly after the erection of the village war memorial which was paid for by public subscription at a cost of £250. The Hotham Inn is on the right in this view. Just at the back of the war memorial was the former site of the village workhouse. It was in use until 1837 when Hotham joined the Howdenshire Poor Law Union. Thereafter, any paupers from the village were sent to a central workhouse in Howden.

Right, a group of local children posing for this photograph taken in c.1910. In 1923 a parish hall was erected on land on the left in this view. Over the years the hall held many social functions but it is best remembered by the older inhabitants of Hotham for the 'tanner hop' dances which were held every Saturday night from 8-11 p.m. The hall was demolished in 1953 to allow for the building of the Westfield Close council estate development. After its demolition part of the old school served as a temporary village hall until 1967 when a new purpose built hall was erected nearby.

Right, Mr. Norman Johnson has been sweeping chimneys in the district for over 30 years. Norman also offers his presence at weddings to uphold the tradition that if a bride sees a chimney sweep it will bring her good luck. He believes this tradition dates back to medieval days when a certain King of England's carriage was travelling along a highway when the horses bolted. A passing chimney sweep, carrying his brushes over his shoulder was crossing the path of the carriage and raising the brushes above his head, he bravely stood his ground and stopped the horses in their tracks. So amazed and delighted was the king that he thanked the sweep, gave him a groat and declared that for ever after all sweeps would be deemed lucky.

Above, this photograph taken in the village hall in 1952 shows founder member and the first President of the Women's Institute, Mrs. Vivien Clitherow about to switch on the first electric light in Hotham. Colonel Clitherow is seated in the immediate foreground on the right. The W. I. was formed in Hotham in 1946 and met in the village hall. It flourished in this small community for many years until 1997 when it was disbanded owing to lack of members.

Above, members of the Hotham W. I. celebrating at the Londesborough Arms Hotel, Market Weighton in January 1973. Back row, left to right, Olive Hyde, Betty Herdman, Violet Davey, Kath Gospel, Julie Johnson, Edna Copeland, Diane Wilson, Connie Lawson. Middle row, left to right, Nellie Grisewood, Marion Sutton, Florence Mitchell, Mrs. Wilkinson, Bella Willis, Peggy Willis. Front row, left to right, Ann Hall, Jean Wilson, Joan Gregory, Hilda Wilson, Val Wilson.

This photograph taken in the early 1950s shows villagers enjoying themselves at one of the annual dances which were held in the village hall to raise money for charitable organisations. This particular dance was held in order to raise money for the newly formed Hotham Cricket Club.

Left, Dunnaby Hall, a 156 acre farm is thought to date from at least 1730 and is presumably named after the Donnby or Dunby family, who were landowners in Hotham in the 13th and 14th centuries. Despite the rather grand name, it would appear that the property has never been anything other than a farmhouse. The small stone farmhouse is believed to be 18th century but enlarged in the 19th. Edward Lawson farmed here from 1907 until c.1940. Left, Edward's children Ginny, Edie, Hannah and young Edward Lawson. During the Second World War a Halifax Mk5 aircraft from the 76th Squadron based at Tollingham aerodrome (about 3 minutes flying time from Hotham), crashed in the fold yard of the farm. The crew baled out but the pilot F/Sgt Frith who stayed at the controls was killed. The cause was thought to have been a build up of snow and ice on the wings of the aeroplane.

Right, Mr. Henry Atkinson the village blacksmith outside his premises c.1930. On the opposite side of the road a small step is just visible. This was at the entrance to Robert James Pearson's shop. A wheelwright, joiner and undertaker by trade he was known locally as 'Tin Bob'. He opened his shop during the mid 1890s and retired about 1930. Robert's sister-in-law Mildred also worked as a wheelwright in the village as did his widowed mother Elizabeth. Incredibly, Elizabeth was still working in that occupation in 1901 at the age of 75. In his spare time Robert played in the South Cave Subscription Silver Band.

Above, a drawing by Frederick Schultz Smith (1860-1925) and dated 1898, showing the northern end of Hotham's Main Street, (formerly known as Church Street). On the right in the drawing is a small grocery shop which was run by William Parrot Dean from c.1909-1920. His daughter Hannah and her husband Thomas Fisher then took over the business.

Above, one of Hotham's oldest residents is Mr. Alf Adamson, seen here with his faithful dog Tan. For many years Alf ran a grocery store with his wife Mary in the Main Street.

Above, this photograph taken in the 1930s shows Hannah Fisher standing outside her general store. Mr. Burfield's post office and stationery shop can be seen just beyond it. Following Hannah's retirement in 1944, Alf Adamson and his wife Mary took over the business. The shop stocked everything imaginable from general groceries through to rabbit snares, ferret muzzles and iron grates. In addition Alf started a mobile shop in 1957 travelling round the district selling groceries and produce which he had grown on the small holding behind the shop. The introduction of supermarket stores and the increasing ownership of private motor cars resulted in Alf's mobile shop becoming no longer viable and consequently he ceased running it by 1961. In 1969 Alf and Mary's shop and two other properties in the block were condemned by Howden Council and they were demolished shortly afterwards. Alf and Mary reopened their shop at what is now number 22, Main Street. Four years later in March 1973 they took the decision to close due to Mary's failing health and increasing loss of customers to the expanding supermarkets. Thereafter, Alf concentrated on hiring himself out for local gardening work and growing vegetable and salad produce for the wholesale market, Humber Street, Hull.

In 1848 there was a Church schoolroom for mixed children and infants in the village. In 1874 the old schoolroom and the adjoining schoolmaster's cottage were demolished and replaced by a new mixed school building and attached schoolmaster's cottage on the same site. The school was enlarged in 1912 in order to accommodate some 60 pupils. By 1948 numbers had fallen to only 26 pupils and in 1949 shortly after this photograph was taken, the village school closed and the children were transferred to schools at Newport and later, Market Weighton. On the back row far left is Amy Burns, infant teacher at the school from 1919 until its closure in 1949. On the far right is Mrs. Harrison the junior teacher. The two up and two down school house which adjoined the school had been let for some time as Mrs. Burns the schoolmistress lived elsewhere in the village. The school room and attached schoolmaster's house still stand but were converted into a private house by Mr. and Mrs. Walberton in 1966.

Above, looking along Main Street from St. Oswald's Church. On the right is Church Farm and a little further down on the left two 'Airy Houses'. Three pairs of these semi-detached houses (constructed of concrete), were built in the village following the end of the Second World War. In November 1987 the owner of one of the above properties paid £15,910 to replace the original concrete shell of the house with brick. Other private owners quickly followed suit and the council replaced the concrete on the remaining properties which it still owned.

St. Oswald's Church

The Church of St. Oswald is situated at the northern end of the long Main Street and is dedicated to St. Oswald. The Church consists of a chancel, north chapel, south porch and a low square western tower, the lower portion being of the Norman period. The surviving fabric suggests that the church was built in the 12th century.

The register dates from 1706 and the following interesting entry was made in it by the Reverend James Stillingfleet in 1790,

"The Reverend John Wesley preached here at 9 o'clock in the morning at the age of 85 years after having preached twice in the High Church at Hull the preceeding day and went hence to preach at Market Weighton at 11 a.m., at Pocklington at 2 p.m. and at York in the evening of this day 4 times."

St. Oswald's has been repaired and restored on numerous occasions over the centuries. In 1904 extensive renovations took place which included the removal of the box pews. A new organ chamber and vestry were built and a two-manual organ installed. The tower was also restored and the two bells hung within it were recast as one bell.

An unusual feature of the church is the elevated loft or pew which was also added in 1904, and built for the exclusive use of the family of the local squire. Reached by a private staircase it has its own fireplace and balcony. A window in the vestry contains fragments of stained glass from York Minster which had been removed in 1840 following a fire in the Minster.

The churchyard was enlarged in 1866 and a burial ground on the opposite side of the road was opened in 1903 including a private cemetery for the Stracey-Clitherow family.

Above top, the exterior of the newly restored Church taken in 1905. St. Oswald's Chuch most prominent feature is the short and very broad Norman western tower. Above, an interior view following the 1904 refurbishments, including the Squire family's special elevated pew.

During the Second World War the church narrowly escaped destruction when a number of surplus bombs and landmines from enemy raids over Hull's docklands, exploded in and around Hotham and North Cave. William Parrott Dean, whose descendents still reside in Hotham "tolled the bell" for over 46 years and was also a village shopkeeper.

St. Oswald's longest surviving charity was provided by Cecil Sabine, who, in his will, proved in 1873, left £500 for bread, clothing and coal for the poor and for the maintenance of his family's graves. The upkeep of the graves was discontinued and in 1920 the entire income was applied to the poor of the parish. In 1997-98 £443 stock produced an income of £11, which was distributed to elderly residents of Hotham, resulting in a handout of eleven £1 doles.

The grand reopening of St. Oswald's Church took place on Saturday, 18th February 1905. His Grace, William Dalrymple MacLagan, The Archbishop of York, rededicated the Church.

A 17th century parsonage house built of stone and thatch was destroyed by fire. John Reid, vicar of Hotham 1710-22 rebuilt the house on the western side of Main Street. It consisted of two lower and two upper rooms. In 1772-3 the house was enlarged and let as Rectory Farm but by 1818 it was considered unfit for habitation. The above property was built in 1775 by Reverend James Stillingfleet, rector 1771-1826 and is situated to the rear of the church. The Reverend John Wesley, M.A. the great evangelist stayed here as a guest of Reverend Stillingfleet in 1788. In 1870 the house was known as Hotham Villa and was purchased to serve as the rectory. It was sold in 1955 and the rector has since lived in the vicarage in Church Street, North Cave where he serves both parishes.

Above, Mill Farm's last summer, before it was demolished in 1988. Ken and Mary Fisher were the last tenant farmers at Mill Farm. They retired in July 1988 after 18 years of farming there. To the right is a photograph taken c.1890 and shows members of the Lawson family who were farmers here from 1871 until 1924 when Henry Pashby Lawson left to take on the larger Church Farm in nearby Main Street. A water-mill for corn existed here in the early 17th century. William Stather was miller and farmer here in the mid 19th century. By 1870, however, the mill had fallen into disuse and was later demolished. The mill-house survived until the farm was demolished.

SELECT BIBLIOGRAPHY

The main documentary sources used were as follows:

East Riding of Yorkshire Council Archive Services, Beverley.

CD12   Civil Defence Incident Book.
DDX   Howdenshire Church Magazines, 1906-1915.
PC16   South Cave Parish Records.
PC38   Hotham Parish Records.
TTBF   Brough Ferry-Newbald Turnpike Records.

Newspapers and Periodicals.

Around The Wolds, Beverley Target, Country Matters, Eastern Morning News, Dalesman, Haltemprice Herald, Hull Advertiser, Hull Daily Mail, Hull News, Hull Packet, Hull Star, Hull Times, The Journal, Yorkshire Archeological Journal, Yorkshire and North Humberside Times, Yorkshire Post, Yorkshire Ridings Magazine.

Unpublished Material.

Alf Adamson, Biographical notes on his life.
Dr. John Branch, (ed.), Life in the Caves 1790-1940, produced by W.E.A. Local History Class, South Cave.
David Neave, (Compiler), Notes on Hotham Hall and its owners, 1976.
Dorothy Roberts, An interview on cassette tape with Frank Warcup, a local resident of South Cave, 1983.
Archie Ernest Trout's Diaries, Volumes 1-4, 1916-1923.
Edwin A.R. Trout, The Biography of A. E. Trout, 1994.
Edwin A.R. Trout, The Publications of A. E. Trout, 1994.
The deposited papers of William Richardson and Archie E. Trout, Local Studies Library, Hull Central Library.

Printed Works.

R. C. & J. D. Anderson, *Quicksilver, A hundred years of coaching 1750-1850, 1973.*
J. Allen, *The Stranger's Guide to Ferriby, Welton, Elloughton and South Cave, 1841.*
K. J. Allison, 'South Cave' in K. J. Allison (ed), *Victoria County History, East Riding, Vol. IV 1979.*
P. Carver, *The Parish Church of St. Oswald, Hotham, 1973.*
P. Carver, (Compiler), *North Cave, A look at our heritage, 1978.*
P. Carver, *All Saints' Church, North Cave, 1975.*
J. E & P. A. Crowther, *The Diary of Robert Sharp of South Cave, Life in a Yorkshire Village 1812-1837, 1997.*
C. Goode. *Railways of East Yorkshire, 1982.*
J. G. Hall, *A History of South Cave and Other Parishes, 1892.*
Hull City Museums Publication No. 17, Building the Hull & Barnsley Railway 1885-1985.
Hull and East Riding Trade Directories 1823-1937.
N. Loughlin & K. R. Miller. *Archaeological Sites in Humberside, 1979.*
G. G. MacTurk, *Notes on South Cave Church and the recent discoveries there, 1882.*
D. Neave, *East Riding Friendly Societies, 1988.*
D. Neave & D. Turnbull, *Landscaped Parks and Gardens of East Yorkshire, 1992.*
D. Neave (ed.), *South Cave, a Market Village Community in the 18th and 19th Centuries, 1974.*
J. Nicholson, *Beacons of the East Riding, 1887.*
R. Rowarth, *A Short Guide to South Cave.*
W. Richardson, *Parish Registers of South Cave, 1909.*
W. Richardson, *Some East Yorkshire Worthies, 1914.*
D. Roberts, (Compiler), *A Short History of All Saints' Church, South Cave, 1979.*
T. Thompson, *A History of Welton and Neighbouring Villages, 1869.*
Colonel White & W. Lambert, *Records of the East Yorkshire Volunteer Force, 1920.*

Articles

R. A. Alec-Smith, 'Cave Castle', The Georgian Society for East Yorkshire Transactions. Vol. IV. Part III. 1956-58.
A. E. Trout, 'An Old Yorkshire Congregation: South Cave Congregational Church', Transactions of the Congregational Historical Society, Sept, 1931.
G. G. MacTurk, 'Denudation in the South Cave District' Hull Geology Society, Vol VI, 1901-1925.
'Visiting The Caves - South Cave & North Cave' Yorkshire Ridings Magazine, Aug/Sept, 1986.